Plum Island

Great Neck

Little Neck

Ipswich Bay

Castle Hill

Fox Creek Canal

Crane Beach

Ipswich

Choate
or
Hog Island

Chebacco
Boat

133

Essex River

Essex
Inc. 1819

Gloucester

Hamilton
Inc. 1793

Chebacco
Lake

N

Wenham

Manchester by-the-sea

Ipswich

STORIES FROM THE RIVER'S MOUTH

Town Memoirs (toun mem'-wärs). 1. True stories that capture the spirit of a community, its genius loci. 2. Anecdotes passed on within a community from generation to generation. 3. A series of books by regional storytellers, illustrated by local artists, preserving the popular history of great American towns.

Ipswich

STORIES FROM THE RIVER'S MOUTH

A MASSACHUSETTS TOWN MEMOIR

BY SAM SHERMAN • Illustrated by Alec Gillman

COMMONWEALTH EDITIONS

Beverly, Massachusetts

❖ DEDICATION ❖

For Keith, Megan, Michael, and Stephanie,
who will make their own history

Library of Congress Cataloging-in-Publication Data
Sherman, Sam, 1961–
    Ipswich: stories from the river's mouth / by Sam Sherman; illustrated by
    Alec Gillman. p. cm. -- (Town memoirs)
    Includes bibliographical references.
    ISBN 1-889833-25-8 (alk. paper)
    1. Ipswich (Mass.)--History--Anecdotes. 2. Ipswich (Mass.)--History--
    Chronology. I. Title. II. Series.
    F74.I6 S43 2001
    974.4'5--dc21

                                                            2001047029

Town Memoirs
Series editor: Liz Nelson
Series designer: Jill Feron/Feron Design
Printed in the United States of America.

Commonwealth Editions is an imprint of Memoirs Unlimited, Inc.,
21 Lothrop Street, Beverly, Massachusetts 01915.

Visit our web site at www.commonwealtheditions.com.

❖ CONTENTS ❖

Nineteenth Century

TWENTIETH CENTURY

❖ ACKNOWLEDGMENTS ❖

Thanks to friends and family for their interest, ideas, and inspiration: Nancy Knights; Gail Forsyth-Vail; Jeanine Black; Eve Hamlin; Robin & Rick Silverman; Bob Van Twuyver.

Many thanks also to the staff of the Ipswich Public Library; Paul Allen of River's Edge Card & Gift Shop; Courtney Peckham of the Essex Shipbuilding Museum; folks at the Ipswich Historical Society, especially Pat Tyler Turner; Bette Savage; John Dolan; Jean Moss.

To those who had an active hand in this book-producing process: thanks to publisher Webster Bull and editor Liz Nelson for the opportunity to write a real book; further thanks to Liz for her artful combination of encouragement and commiseration (with a hefty dose of humor) through this whole adventure. Thanks also to Karen Marzlow for her attentive copyediting efforts. And many thanks to Alec Gillman for his insight and his illustrations, bringing this Ipswich history to life with the touch of his pen.

1633	Official settlement of Agawam by party led by John Winthrop Jr. (1606–1676)
1634	Town incorporated as Ipswich
1638	Town land purchased from Masconomet
1650	Land trust for support of Ipswich Grammar School established with five feoffees chosen to oversee trust
1679	Chebacco parish formed
1687	Ipswich men speak out against colonial governor's decree for tax collection
1700	Population of Ipswich approximately 1,800
1715	The Hamlet parish formed
1764	Stone bridge built over Ipswich River and named for Col. John Choate (1697–1765)
1790	Ipswich women produce and sell 41,979 yards of lace
1790	First United States census lists Ipswich population as 4,562
1793	The Hamlet incorporated as the town of Hamilton
1819	Chebacco incorporated as the town of Essex
1838	Lighthouse constructed on Ipswich beach
1868	Ipswich Mills Company begins manufacturing hosiery
1900	Population of Ipswich listed as 4,658
1917	Cable Hospital opened
1927	First Crane mansion at Castle Hill completed
1928	Ipswich Mills Company closed
1950	Paleo-Indian artifacts discovered near Bull Brook
1997	Three Catholic parishes—St. Joseph, Sacred Heart, St. Stanislaus—merged to form Our Lady of Hope
2000	Population of Ipswich listed as 12,987

Ipswich

STORIES FROM THE RIVER'S MOUTH

SEVENTEENTH CENTURY

Ipswich in the Seventeenth Century

The verdant hills and teeming waters of the river and sea made the "agawam" a favorite summering place of the native people. The natural resources attracted English settlers as well, and it was here near the mouth of the river that they established Ipswich, a town prominent in the Massachusetts Bay Colony, in large part because of its influential residents. Its founders were Puritans, and the strict tenets of their religion governed virtually every aspect of life in the seventeenth-century town.

❖

JOHN WINTHROP JR.: SO MUCH TO DO . . .

The breeze off the ocean had the lingering nip of winter as it pushed the small sailing vessel into the mouth of the river. The men on board, huddled deep into their woolen cloaks, shifted restlessly, knowing they had nearly reached their destination. Their leader, John Winthrop Jr., son of the colonial governor, eyed the promise and the challenge of the March landscape. This is where they would plant their town.

The natives described this abundant fishing ground as the "agawam." The English found the word efficient to label both the location and the people. In the early spring of 1633, Winthrop and a dozen other men built their first crude shelters between a bend in the river that would become the wharf area and the hill where they would construct the meetinghouse of Agawam. There was much work to do with building and planting and preparing their new homes for their families waiting in Boston; Winthrop, full of eagerness and energy at twenty-seven, was up to the task.

Colonial leaders believed that settling to the north of Salem would keep the French from expanding their holdings into these desirable regions. The early going was far from comfortable, and the threats of wilderness living made the settlers uneasy. Winthrop soon wrote to his father, requesting muskets and other arms.

Martha Winthrop was reluctant to join her husband in the new settlement—the location was so wild and remote, the house so rude, and the town lacking in the comforting and civilizing influence of a minister—but she finally arrived in November. Her husband, excited by new ideas and endeavors, probably reveled in all of the conditions that she found disheartening. His enthusiasm made him a popular leader among his neighbors and his presence kept their morale high.

Misfortune was not long in visiting the young settlement. In August 1634 Martha Winthrop and her infant daughter died; they were likely the first settlers to be laid to rest in the town's burying ground.

There is no way of knowing across the span of nearly four hundred years what effect this had on the young husband and father. By October he departed Ipswich for England. His neighbors sorely missed his leadership and inspiration, for he was absent about a year, and when he returned to New England, he had with him a new wife—eighteen-year-old Elizabeth Reade—and a new project: he had been commissioned by Lords Say and Brook to establish another settlement, this time in Connecticut.

From that time on, Winthrop's presence in Ipswich was never constant, although other residents tried to lure him with parcels of land, including Castle Hill. He wasn't any more consistent with his other obligations. Though he was in charge of guiding the construction of a fort and settlement at Saybrook, he seems to have spent much of that year in Boston (where his wife and parents were). He was a member of the Massachusetts Court of Assistants, but he often missed sessions while in Ipswich or Connecticut. In 1638, he proposed to move to Ryall Side in Salem (later part of Beverly) to establish a saltworks; then in 1641 he was off to England to seek backing for an ironworks in Braintree. By the late 1640s he and his family had settled in Connecticut, where he became governor in 1657.

Winthrop had trained for the law in London, but he was also greatly interested in science and was a practicing physician. He wrote on shipbuilding and beer brewing, made explorations as a fur trader and prospector, and taught a blind woman in Ipswich to read using letters carved in wood. In later life he pursued astronomy and chemistry. A correspondent of great scientific minds of his day, including Sir Christopher Wren and Sir Isaac Newton, Winthrop has been called "America's first scientist." Perhaps some aura of his curiosity and quest for knowledge lingers in the air of Ipswich's Winthrop Elementary School, inspiring students nearly four centuries later.

❖

MASCONOMET

Masconomet, a sagamore, or chief, of the local Native Americans called the Agawams by the English, met John Winthrop the Elder when Winthrop arrived aboard the *Arbella* in 1630. Masconomet and one of his men boarded the ship and spent the day with Winthrop and others of the Massachusetts Bay Company.

He had met Englishmen before. Masconomet had welcomed Capt. Edward Hardie and Nicholas Hobson nearly twenty years earlier, when the travelers, bound for a place they called Virginia, had stopped only for a short time. Those Englishmen had seen the plentiful times, when Masconomet's people had been many and their territory had been large. Their wigwams dotted the landscape and their corn grew tall. They stayed often at the "agawam," the place where great schools of fish ran, that the Englishmen would come to call Ipswich.

In the intervening years Masconomet's people had been decimated by plague and warfare. Those remaining lived in fear of attack by the Tarrantines, their enemies from the coast of what would become Maine. To protect the dwindling population of his tribe, the pragmatic leader allied himself with the newcomers who were settling in the region. Their first governor, John Endicott, sent men to defend the Agawams when the sagamore heard rumors of an attack by the Tarrantines. Masconomet hoped that John Winthrop, the new governor, would also look kindly on his people.

Bit by bit Masconomet ceded his territory to the Puritans. He officially sold the land of Ipswich to John Winthrop Jr. in 1638, five years after the initial settlement of the town and four years after its incorporation. He received twenty pounds as payment.

Although Masconomet was recognized early on as friendly to the settlers, in 1631 the sagamore was barred from the houses of all Englishmen for the span of a year on the penalty of a ten-beaver-skin fine as a sanction for having led an attack on a

Masconomet officially sold the land of Ipswich to John Winthrop Jr. in 1638, five years after the initial settlement of the town and four years after its incorporation.

Tarrantine village. Ten years later, when vague rumors of an impending uprising spread through the colonial towns, all natives of the region were stripped of their guns, which had been provided by the English for hunting. Once the gossip died down, the guns were returned.

By 1644 Masconomet and other remaining sagamores accepted that life as they had known it was gone forever. They signed a document putting themselves, their people, and their lands under the jurisdiction of the Massachusetts Bay Colony and promised to receive instruction in the teachings of Christianity. Once again, Masconomet and the others took the pragmatic view. When asked if they would worship God and refrain from blasphemy, their response was recorded as: "We do desire to reverence the God of the English, and to speak well of him, because we see He doth better to the English than other gods do to others."

The shrinking population of native residents came under the care of the town. Some, like Masconomet, were granted small parcels of land. He received six acres in 1655—all that remained of his once extensive territory. When he died three years later, he was buried in the tradition of his tribe, despite his conversion to Christianity.

In 1667, three young men went on a tear through town. They vandalized several bridges and desecrated the grave of Masconomet, digging up some of the bones and carrying the skull on a stick. They were fined and jailed for several days, then displayed in the stocks and ordered to gather up the sagamore's remains and re-inter them in a new grave "with a cover of stones upon it two feet high." Masconomet lies buried at a place named for him, Sagamore Hill, now part of Hamilton.

❖

WRECK OF THE *WATCH AND WAIT*

Anthony Thacher and his cousin John Avery stood on the wharf at Ipswich as the crew of the pinnace *Watch and Wait* made ready to sail. The small vessel, owned by Isaac Allerton, made regular trips along the coast carrying goods and passengers between Piscataqua and Boston; on this August Wednesday the Thacher and Avery families were bound from Ipswich to Marblehead. The two men watched their lively band of children scamper about the wharf as their household goods were loaded and their wives prepared to board.

The cousins had made a pact during their voyage from England to remain together in the New World, settling in the same place and standing by each other through good times and bad. Avery, who had served as a minister in England, was approached to take on a new church in Marblehead. He had originally declined the invitation and went instead to Newbury where he and Thacher considered taking up farming. But members of the Massachusetts Bay clergy finally persuaded him to accept the Marblehead position.

On August 12, 1635, the Averys and their nine children, the Thachers and their four children, their maidservant, and one other passenger named William Elliott set sail on the *Watch and Wait* with a four-man crew. The boat made its way down the Ipswich River to the bay. Southward progress along the coast was extremely slow as a stiff headwind rose, forcing the vessel's crew to tack endlessly back and forth. By Friday, August 14, the vessel still had not rounded Cape Ann.

That night the wind swelled to a gale then shifted direction. By midnight a strong nor'easter was battering the pinnace and tearing at its sails. The wind and rain raged so fiercely and the night gathered around them so darkly that the sailors couldn't go aloft to rig new sails or furl the torn ones. The captain dropped anchor and decided to ride out the storm until morning. The heaving seas made short work of the anchorage, and the boat was cast adrift at the mercy of the pounding waves.

Passengers and crew alike huddled in the cabin as water poured over the decks. Suddenly, the sea tossed the vessel onto a jagged ledge, smashing the bow on the rocks. The masts snapped like twigs, and the hull broke open. One of the sailors was washed overboard only to be carried back again as a wave surged into the cabin and tossed him into Thacher's arms. The marooned voyagers could make out the silhouette of nearby land—temptingly close— and the sailor jumped overboard once more to swim for it. The captain also decided to brave the elements and clambered up on deck for a better look. Both men disappeared into the teeth of the storm and were never seen again.

Then, before the passengers had a chance to catch their breaths, another wave crashed over them. Thacher, his daughter Mary, Avery, and his eldest son were swept out of the cabin and onto the rocks. Mrs. Thacher was tossed into the sea. Thacher's three younger children huddled together, and he saw their pale, frightened faces clearly before another wave shattered the remains of the pinnace and engulfed all those still aboard. That same wave knocked Thacher and the others from their precarious footing on the ledge.

Thacher struggled in the churning waters, which literally tore the clothes from his body, until he finally landed on a small island where, by some good fortune, his wife had also managed to escape the sea. All the other passengers and crew of the *Watch and Wait* were lost. The stunned couple searched in vain for other survivors and gathered the few provisions washed up from the wreckage. Thacher found a flint and steel as well as a powder horn containing enough dry powder to make a fire, and they recovered several articles of clothing. Cheese and a drowned goat provided them with food, and they sustained themselves until Monday afternoon when a passing boat spotted and rescued them.

Thacher was later granted the island. He named it Thacher's Woe (Thachers Island today) and the nearby rock Avery's Fall.

Avery's eldest daughter, the only victim recovered from the wreck, was buried on the island.

THE NOT-SO-SIMPLE GENTLEMAN OF AGAWAM

The Reverend Nathaniel Ward had left behind in England both good times and bad. A minister's son whose two brothers followed in their father's footsteps, young Nathaniel broke with tradition by becoming a lawyer. Later, he traveled extensively through Europe and, in Heidelberg, met David Pareus, an illustrious theologian who inspired him to take up the ministry even though he was already over forty years old. As rector at Stondon Massey, Ward gained a reputation as a nonconformist. His unbending Puritan views were at odds with the English theocracy, and after ten years in the pulpit he was excommunicated. Around this time Ward's wife passed away. (Yes, somewhere amidst his work, travels, and studies he had married, though nothing is known about the woman in question.)

The following year, 1634, Ward embarked for America and the great Puritan experiment in the Massachusetts Bay Colony. Fortunately for him, he emigrated before the English government issued a proclamation forbidding ministers to travel to the colonies without permission from the archbishop of Canterbury. He may have anticipated difficulty leaving England; there is no record of his passage, which may indicate that he tried to be elusive and succeeded.

Ward's keen mind and broad experience in both law and the ministry made him a valuable addition to the society of Massachusetts Bay. He was drawn to Ipswich by the caliber of its other residents, the dynamic leadership of John Winthrop Jr., and the town's need for a minister.

Despite the righteousness of his mission, the Reverend Mr. Ward was often daunted by the rigors of his new life in the rugged coastal town. His health suffered under the demands of the climate and the privations of the colony. He spent his first winter in Winthrop's house while the town's founder was in England, and in one letter to him Ward described himself as "tender and more unfit for solitariness and hardship than some other." Although his three children had joined him in New England, they were all pursuing their own lives in the new land: James, the youngest, attended Harvard College; Susan married Giles Firmin, a physician in Ipswich; and the eldest, John, joined a number of other Ipswich men in settling Haverhill, where he became minister (Ward Hill is named for him). After three years, Nathaniel Ward's delicate condition forced him to resign as pastor.

Stepping down from the pulpit did not mean retirement for Mr. Ward. His great learning, experience in the law, and gift for writing made him a perfect choice for the committee formed to codify the laws of the colony. After three years' labor, Ward presented his work to the General Court, the Massachusetts Bay colonial government. The code of one hundred laws—called the Body of Liberties—was sent to all the towns in the colony for their consideration. It was officially adopted in 1641.

Even though he was intensely involved in the workings of the colony, Ward took as great an interest in events unfolding in old England. At this time his native land was in a state of civil war with an ongoing power struggle between the monarchy and the leaders of Parliament. After completing the Body of Liberties, Ward switched literary gears and addressed the political and religious issues of England in a satire titled, *The Simple Cobler of Aggawam*. The "cobler" was, according to the book's title page, "willing to help mend his Native Country, lamentably tattered, both in the upper-leather and sole, with all the honest stitches he can take." The fictional shoemaker took on a whole range of topics in his biting commentary, from religious tolerance and the current political strife in England to men's hair and women's fashion. How much of the curmudgeonly "cobler" was in his creator and vice versa, we'll never know.

The Simple Cobler was published in London in 1647 and met with great success. The not-so-simple gentleman of Agawam ended his adventure in the colony and returned to England around the time the book was published (the religious climate had eased since his departure). He continued to write until his death in 1653.

❖

THE POET'S FAMILY

When twenty-three-year-old Anne Bradstreet settled in Ipswich in 1635, she came as part of an extended family that added several new households to the fledgling town. Her own household consisted of her husband Simon, their son Samuel, and their infant daughter Dorothy. Anne's brother Samuel Dudley had married Mary Winthrop, daughter of the colonial governor and sister of John Winthrop Jr., and the couple took up a farm in the part of Ipswich called Chebacco (now Essex). Her sister Patience was newly married to Daniel Denison, who would become a prominent Ipswich citizen and distinguished military figure. Anne's parents, Dorothy and Thomas Dudley (who was serving as deputy governor at the time he took up residence in Ipswich), lived next door to the Bradstreets with their two youngest daughters, Sarah and Mercy.

Anne had already begun expressing herself through poetry, but her creative endeavors flourished in this close community of family and interesting, influential friends. Among the Bradstreets' neighbors were Richard Saltonstall and Nathaniel Ward, men of ideas and influence in the life of the town and the colony. Saltonstall, who, along with Anne's brother-in-law Daniel Denison, served as a deputy of the Massachusetts General Court, was a fiery young magistrate and keen debater of democratic issues. His wife Muriel was just about Anne's age. Of particular influence on Anne was old Nathaniel Ward, who may have reminded Anne of her father; the two men were similar in their staunch Puritan outlook as well as their kind encouragement of Anne's intellectual and creative pursuits.

The Ipswich enclave of family grew and changed and drifted apart in just a few short years. In 1638, the Bradstreets' third child, Sarah, was born. That same year Anne's youngest sisters married and moved away. After the marriages, Anne's parents also left Ipswich and settled in Roxbury, and brother Samuel departed to help establish the new settlement of Salisbury.

Anne's work was inspired as much by the absence of family members as by their presence. Many of her poems addressed to Simon were written during his frequent trips to Boston on colonial government business. And after her parents moved to Roxbury in 1638, Anne often addressed and sent works to her father. She also wrote a poetic "Epitaph" to her mother, who died in 1643.

It wasn't until after the Bradstreets moved to Andover that Anne saw her poetry published, but this turn of events also had its roots in her Ipswich circle of friends and family. They had been Anne's intended audience for her poetry; she had never aspired to publish her writings. But, unbeknownst to Anne, her brother-in-law John Woodbridge took her poems to Nathaniel Ward's publisher in London, and Ward wrote the introduction to the collection. Anne's book, *The Tenth Muse Lately Sprung up in America,* was published, and enthusiastically received, in 1650.

❖

THERE AROSE SUCH A CLATTER

Good pranksters have a knack for making the most of the elements at hand. Brothers Thomas and John Manning found a fitting target in Mark Quilter, a cowherd who enjoyed his drink. They engineered a bit of mischief that made use of one of the creatures tended by Quilter as well as the features of seventeenth-century house construction.

Families of modest means like the Quilters lived in single-story homes, which allowed easy access to the roofs. Chimneys were made of wood daubed with clay, and they were constructed with

A low roof, a large chimney, a small calf—
the ingredients of a worthy prank.

wide openings in order to minimize the chance of sparks' and embers' making contact with the chimney walls.

A low roof, a large chimney, a small calf—the ingredients of a worthy prank! Tom and John must have been hard pressed not to laugh out loud as they mounted Mark Quilter's roof in the dark of night, trying to hold tight to a leggy young heifer while keeping their purchase on the steep incline. They dropped the bewildered animal down the dark maw of the chimney.

Unfortunately, the fate of the calf was not recorded, but imagine it landing a good kick to the ribs of one of the pranksters as they tried to contain its gangly legs. Hear it bawling in protest during its short drop down the chimney, its hooves clattering on the hearthstones and scattering the ashes as it touched down. Likely, a collision occurred as it bounded out of the fireplace just as Mark Quilter leapt from his bed with an astounded exclamation. With any luck, after a few excited hops around the room, the disoriented creature found freedom and familiar territory when its equally bewildered master opened the door.

❖

A DOG'S LIFE

Some laws of early Ipswich applied to the dogs of the town rather than to the human inhabitants. Many of a dog's comings and goings were legislated, making it difficult for a trusty companion to accompany his human as he went about work or worship. It was decreed that no dog "nor yet more a swine" was allowed in the meetinghouse "if it could possibly be prevented."

The cornfields were off limits, as many dogs liked to dig up the fish used for fertilizer. A town vote in May 1644 required all dogs to have one leg tied up to keep the animals close to home and away from the corn for three weeks after the posting of the law. If a dog broke loose, his master was required to pay damages. Those masters refusing to tie their dogs were required to pay a fine plus any damages done by Rover.

Humans were also strict about dogs harassing flocks of sheep. A 1642 law stated that the owner would have to pay double damages if his dog killed a sheep, and the dog would be hanged immediately. The hanging of dogs took on a more sinister tone later in the century, when a number were sent to the gallows on suspicion of witchcraft.

❖

REGULATING ROMANCE

Many of the activities of private life were matters for the court in early Ipswich. Personal relationships were never to be decided solely by the man and woman involved. Seeking to marry a woman "without the consent of her friends" was against the law (presumably this was to protect women who had no parents or other relatives to look out for their interests in such a situation). It was against the law to court a girl without her parents' consent. Even with a courtship underway, it was against the law to engage in "making love"—that is, affectionate activity of any description—outside the bonds of marriage.

This much regulation of romance might seem intrusive, but it sometimes proved enlightening. During the quarterly court session in Ipswich in November 1649, a ladies' man named Matthew Stanley was charged with "drawing away the affections" of John Tarbox's daughter without her parents' permission. On the very same day Stanley was also found guilty of fornication with another young woman, Ruth Andrews. The couple (Stanley and Andrews) was sentenced to be whipped or to pay a fine of fifty shillings. The sentence would not be carried out, however, if they got married.

BUILDING A LEGEND

Legends passed down through generations often raise more questions than they answer. Such is the case with the first boat built in the Chebacco section of Ipswich.

The boat was probably built some time during the 1650s, after the first local sawmill opened and before the first shipyard was established in 1668. Legend has it that the boat was built by a man named Burnham and adds the interesting detail that he constructed this historic craft in an upper room of his house.

This is where the legend fails us, for it says nothing about why our pioneer shipbuilder chose such a workshop. Secrecy for his unprecedented endeavor? Lack of a barn? Fear of being caught working on the Sabbath as he toiled obsessively on this wonderful creation? Banishment to the garret by a wife who didn't want his construction cluttering up the main room? We'll never know.

The only other detail the legend provides is that, once completed, the boat was too large and unwieldy to leave the house the same way its component parts had entered, and our carpenter Burnham had to take out a window and part of the wall in order to introduce his newborn boat to the outside world. Perhaps inspired by their ingenious ancestor, generations of Burnhams would be shipbuilders in Chebacco, which later became the town of Essex. In 2001, an Essex Burnham named Harold continues the tradition.

FIRE HAZARD

Fires were a real danger to the homes of the early settlers of Ipswich due largely to the way houses were built. Riskiest of all were thatched roofs and wooden chimneys. With this in mind, the town fathers passed an ordinance in 1642 that all households keep

Drawing near, they saw the smoke and soon saw the flames dancing among the thatch over the chimney.

a ladder near the house in preparation for fighting a fire. Another ordinance, of 1647, required that homeowners inspect their chimneys and keep them clean and free of any cracks or chips in the clay daub covering the wood. Further, in 1649, it was ordered that no haystack be placed within three rods (approximately fifty feet) of a house.

Despite these precautions, Jacob Perkins's home was destroyed by fire in the summer of 1668. One August afternoon Perkins and his wife went into town, leaving their young servant Mehitabel Brabrooke at her chores about the house. She had a kettle boiling over the fire to wash some clothes, and when she wasn't looking, a spark touched off a small flame where a crack in the chimney's clay covering exposed the wood underneath. Mehitabel dipped into the laundry pot and quenched the flame.

Laundry was a hot, tedious task for the sixteen-year-old girl. On such a beautiful summer day, the young woman could think of a long list of things she would rather be doing, and she left the kettle to step outside. She took her pipe with her, thinking to sit a moment and have a smoke. The sight of the tall, green cornstalks waving in the breeze not far from the door reminded her of Master Perkins's red-faced anger when the hogs got into the corn. She thought she had better make sure none of the rooting beasts were in among the rows, but the plants were so tall she needed a better vantage point.

The oven made a fine stepping stool where it bulged out from the broad chimney. She stood on her toes, steadying herself with one hand on the eaves of the thatched roof, and inspected the cornfield. While she searched for movement among the long, green leaves, she took her pipe from her mouth and tapped it against the back of her arm to knock out the ash in order to fill it afresh. There: a stirring in the plants, a hog certainly! Mehitabel had only just climbed down and started toward the hog in the corn when she saw the smoke curling from the roof, right where she had emptied what she thought was a cold pipe.

Mehitabel dropped her pipe and ran to the neighboring house, trying to control her fright and figure out how to get herself out of the trouble she was facing. She reached the house of Abraham Perkins and found his wife, Hannah. Catching her breath, Mehitabel asked Goodwife Perkins if she would mind helping her with the heavy kettle of laundry she was doing. Hannah called her own servant to keep an eye on the children, then started back to Jacob Perkins' house with Mehitabel.

Drawing near, they saw the smoke and soon saw the flames dancing among the thatch near the chimney. While Mehitabel ran to the well for water, Hannah Perkins looked into the open door of the house, noting that the fire had not started in either of the chimneys. She climbed up on the oven, just where Mehitabel had stood, and took the water pail the girl brought to her and threw it on the fire. By this time, though, the flames had taken a strong hold on the roof and were already licking at the walls and chimneys. The fire was beyond containment.

Mehitabel Brabrooke soon found herself facing the Quarterly Court. She was found guilty of "extreme carelessness if not wilfully burning the house." The possibility that she had set the fire purposely arose through the testimony of a young man who had been talking to Mehitabel hours before the fire. Mehitabel had complained that her mistress was angry with her, and the young woman claimed she had exacted her vengeance by putting a toad into the family's milk pail. Mehitabel was sentenced to be whipped and to pay damages to Jacob Perkins.

❖

JUSTICE FOR LIONEL

In 1669, a tired-looking party of Native Americans appeared in Ipswich. Apparently, they were survivors of a massacre and had fled their former home near the headwaters of the Merrimack River. Among the group were an old woman, her son, and her daughter, who had two small sons of her own. Both of the women's husbands had been killed in the attack. The young woman's leg was badly injured.

They set up a wigwam on Castle Hill on land belonging to Daniel Epes, who offered them help when he discovered them there. They spoke very little English, so he called on other Native Americans still living in the area to find out what their circumstances were and to let them know they were welcome to remain on his land. The young woman's health did not improve, and her elderly mother did her best to care for her and the two small boys. Little is said of what the boys' uncle did to provide for his relatives, but Epes described other Native Americans as laughing at his awkwardness and his "Indisposition unto any worke."

About six months after their arrival, the young woman died. On her deathbed she expressed her gratitude to Epes and asked that he look after her older son, who was about three years old; Epes had already taken to calling him Daniel. She also made it clear that she wanted to give him her younger son, who was still an infant. Epes agreed, and his own son Lionel begged that they call the baby Lionel, too. The old woman continued to care for the boys in the wigwam for a number of years. Epes provided them with food, and his servants cut firewood for them and helped move the wigwam between its summer location near Epes's house and its winter shelter among the trees. Nothing more is said about what happened to young Daniel, but Lionel often spent time in Epes's house, though he never moved completely out of the wigwam because his grandmother was afraid to be alone.

When Lionel was about nine, the rest of his family left Ipswich, and Epes expected that the boy would finally live with him. But several weeks later Lionel's uncle reappeared when Epes was away from home and took the youngster with him. The uncle had been gambling on horse races and owed money to Henry Bennett, a farmer who lived not far from Epes. To settle the debt, the uncle sold Lionel to Bennett as an indentured servant for a period of eleven years.

Epes was furious. Bennett claimed he had Lionel legally, with a document signed by the boy's uncle and grandmother. Epes compared the arrangement to someone going to Bennett's home and taking one of his sons to sell; paper or no paper, it would be wrong. He started legal proceedings to nullify the indenture contract and get Lionel back. The suit dragged through the courts and took more than seven years to settle—seven years of servitude for Lionel. The case finally appeared before the Court of Assistants, which reversed the lower court's rulings and allowed Lionel to go home.

❖

CRIMES OF FASHION

In September 1675, a group of women was called before the Quarterly Court at Ipswich. The wives of Shoreborne Wilson, Arthur Abbott, Benedict Pulcipher, John Kindrick, Thomas Knowlton, and Obadiah Bridges, as well as Haniell Bosworth's two daughters and one Margaret Lambert, all appeared before the judges. Their offense? Wearing silk hoods and scarves. All but the wife of Sherborne Wilson, a cooper, were obliged to pay a fine.

Within a few short years of the founding of Ipswich, the sturdy Puritan stock was weakening to the temptations of lace finery and fashions imported from the Continent, much to the chagrin of local leaders. The General Court had defined appropriate garb in the Massachusetts Bay Colony in 1634, drawing the line at lace and embroidery, as well as silver and gold. Wide sleeves and breeches and excessive cuffs were also frowned upon. However, controlling the colonists' appetite for fashion seems to have been beyond the power of even the Court, which tempered its views in the early 1650s. The new proclamation stated that such decorative fashions (while the Court still detested them) could be worn by those individuals whose estates were valued at £200 or more. In other words, the wealthy could befeather and lace themselves as they saw fit, but the common folk were to remain properly plain.

Both women and men were admonished in the Ipswich court for wearing lace. Those, like the cooper Wilson, who could prove that the value of their estate entitled them to wear such decorations, were free to go. The rest were fined for daring to dress above their station.

Fashion policing became a wearisome task for the court, and surely the settlers tired of the topic as well. In 1682 another group of young women ran afoul of the law for "folding their hair, frizzling and knots, and for wearing silk scarves." Although the warrant named ten offenders, only three appeared in court, and their case was dismissed for lack of witnesses.

JUSTICE SWIFT, AND BY THE LETTER

"Stand! Who goes there?"

William Lattimore, Richard Simmons, and John Trevit pulled up their horses, straining their eyes in the gathering darkness of an early March evening to see who was calling to them. Riding north from Boston, they had only just passed George Darling's inn in Salem. The three shadowy figures confronting them spoke again, ordering them off their horses in threatening tones.

Wasting no time, the highwaymen yanked Lattimore from his horse and robbed him of his gold and silver. Two of the robbers began to beat him viciously, but the third pulled them away from him. They dragged Simmons from his mount as well, but he bolted, and they chased him through the woods, cornering him against a tree where they began to beat him. The commotion attracted some of the patrons at Darling's, who ran to the scene and rescued Simmons before the thieves could take the large sum of money that he was carrying.

The travelers and the patrons at the inn identified the highwaymen as Thomas Leonard, Samuel Moore, and Blaze Vinton. The trio was apprehended and charged with robbing on the highway. They appeared before the Ipswich court in March 1677. The graphic testimony of the victims cinched the case, although William Lattimore also spoke up on behalf of Blaze Vinton, who, he said, had kept the other two from beating him to death. The highwaymen were declared guilty, fined, and sentenced to be branded on the forehead. Blaze Vinton's branding was set aside.

The punishment was not uncommon. Also on the docket in Ipswich that March was a case against George Major. Major may have felt his neighbor John Knight had more than ample provisions and would hardly notice if some of his pork and beef went missing. He may simply have been lacking in conscience or over-endowed with greed. Whatever his motivation, Major crept into Knight's house early one morning and took some of the stores hanging from the beams. Although there was a witness to his crime—James, the Knight family's servant—Major denied the theft when he was confronted later that day by one of Knight's sons and a friend. Knight's daughters asked Major's daughter about the meat, and when she in turn asked her mother, she received a slap on the face and harsh instruction not to speak of the matter.

Despite his denials, Major was summoned to court and charged with the crime. With witnesses against him and no one to speak for him—his wife failed to appear because, it was said, she couldn't leave a sick child—he was convicted. The Court ruled that he pay a fine and, like Leonard and Moore, be branded on the forehead with a "B" for "burglar."

The magistrates of the Ipswich court wasted no time in meting out justice. Their sentences didn't include lengthy prison terms, as lawbreakers were expected to pay their penalties and return to their Puritan duty of contributing to society. But criminals might be forever branded by their transgressions in the eyes of their neighbors—literally.

❖

THE GOODWIVES OF CHEBACCO

When Ipswich was first established, residents of Chebacco (now Essex) attended the meetinghouse in the center of Ipswich. Like other outlying settlers, most Chebacco families traveled five miles or more to Sunday morning services, stayed on for the afternoon meeting, then made the return trip home late in the day. This was especially hard in the winter when days were short and cold, although the muddy roads of spring made for hard travel, too.

In February 1677, a number of Chebacco residents gathered at the home of William Cogswell to discuss the possibility of setting up their own meetinghouse. They drafted a petition to the town of Ipswich proposing the plan. The petition came before the town meeting that same month, but it was neither approved nor rejected; the organizers of the meeting simply refused to put it to a vote. The people of Chebacco took the matter to the General Court, but rather than deciding the issue, the Court ordered Ipswich to vote on it at the next year's town meeting.

The following February, the Ipswich town meeting approved a plan for the selectmen to confer with representatives from Chebacco. Several of these meetings were held without result. The Ipswich leaders determined that Chebacco was free to set up its own meetinghouse as long as residents maintained their membership (and their tithing) in the Ipswich church. Needless to say, the Chebacco folk were not eager to take on the financial support of two congregations.

With another winter upon them, the people of Chebacco extended an invitation to the Reverend Jeremiah Shepard to join their community as minister. In January 1679, services in Chebacco began with residents crowded together in a private house. They began discussing the necessity for building a larger structure even as the Reverend Mr. Shepard received an order from the Ipswich church to stop preaching.

On a sunny spring day, with their husbands strangely absent, the women of Chebacco gathered for the raising of the meetinghouse.

Chebacco responded by petitioning the town again, while Ipswich petitioned the General Court, charging the Chebacco residents with defiance—from suspending their tithing in Ipswich to not suspending their Sabbath meetings. In fact, the Chebacco families had stopped the meetings (Shepard may have been a bit frightened of opposing authority), though they had moved ahead with construction of a meetinghouse. The Quarterly Court at Ipswich sided with the town and ordered the men of Chebacco to cease all building until the matter could be resolved.

Goodwives Varney, Martin, and Goodhue agreed that Chebacco residents should follow the letter of the law. The order stated quite clearly that the men were not to erect the meetinghouse, but it said nothing about the womenfolk. Furthermore, it put no restrictions on men from other towns. So, on a sunny spring day, with their husbands strangely absent from the site, the women of Chebacco gathered for the raising of the meetinghouse. They were reinforced by some sturdy men from Gloucester and Manchester.

Not long afterward the Ipswich constable arrived with a warrant for the arrest of the wives of William Goodhue, Thomas Varney, and Abraham Martin. The warrant also called for the arrest of Abraham Martin and his servant John Chubb, who had accompanied Goodwife Martin when she rode to the neighboring towns to ask for assistance. The ringleaders of the plot faced the court in Ipswich and were found guilty of contempt of the previous court order.

The General Court settled the matter once and for all. The guilty parties were instructed to appear at the Salem court on June 24 to publicly acknowledge their wrongdoing. This might have been humiliating except that three weeks earlier the General Court had granted Chebacco's petition for a meetinghouse of its own and appointed a committee to settle the details promptly. In July, the committee approved completion of the meetinghouse and the calling of a new minister.

The minister let the stranger talk him into a bout and indicated an area in front of the parsonage surrounded by a low stone wall as a suitable arena.

❖

THE WRESTLING MINISTER

The Reverend John Wise, first minister of Chebacco parish, arrived at his new post with an unusual reputation. During his youth and his years at Harvard College (he was in all likelihood the first son of an indentured servant to attend the college), the athletic Wise had earned distinction as a wrestler. Although he probably put such competitions aside during his service of two churches before his arrival in Chebacco and while starting a family, a challenge arose not long after his settlement in Ipswich's new church.

A blustery captain from Andover named John Chandler came calling on Wise one afternoon. Chandler, it seems, had run out of competition closer to home but had heard of a minister who might make a worthy opponent. Sure of himself and skeptical of the physical talents of a man of letters and the church, Chandler rode confidently up to Wise's house.

Wise was somewhat surprised by his visitor's challenge to a wrestling match and a bit reluctant to engage him. The thought of what his congregants would say if they saw their minister rolling around on the ground like a common brawler probably went through his mind even as he was sizing up the swaggering Captain Chandler. But the minister let the stranger talk him into a bout and indicated an area in front of the parsonage surrounded by a low stone wall as a suitable arena.

The men squared off, and Wise emerged victorious. Chandler shrugged off the defeat and requested a rematch. Wise proceeded to overpower his opponent again and finished the round with a flourish, tossing the good captain over the wall. Chandler stood up and brushed himself off. With a laugh he thanked Wise for his time and said that if the minister would be so kind as to throw his horse over the wall as well, he would be on his way.

❖

Taxation without representation

When the architects of the American Revolution fiercely decried the heavy-handed laws of England in the 1770s, they followed in the footsteps of Ipswich citizens who had protested the same issue nearly a hundred years earlier.

In the 1680s, England revoked the Massachusetts charter, dissolved the colonial government, and sent Sir Edmund Andros to take over as governor-general. Andros arrived in Boston in December 1686 with an escort of sixty redcoats, a strong military background, and little gift for diplomacy.

The new governor-general's first priority was to revise the code of laws, but to keep operations smooth, he intended to proclaim the old laws in effect until new ones were in place. The recently ousted government had foreseen his intention. In order to humiliate Andros and complicate matters, the General Court had, in one of its last official acts, repealed all the revenue laws of Massachusetts. Andros was forced to act quickly and decreed "An Act for the Continuing and Establishing of several Rates, Duties and Imposts."

The new tax law raised a poll tax on every male resident over the age of sixteen and levied a property tax of a penny per pound of valuation. The act further required each town to appoint a commissioner to collect the taxes on an annual basis.

It was not the taxes themselves that colonists found objectionable. It was the fact that the colonists had no say in the matter. Under the original charter, proposed laws were debated in an assembly of representatives from each town. Suddenly the colonists found themselves with a governor-general who believed that his word was law.

All of the towns in Essex County—with the exception of Salem, Marblehead, and Newbury—protested the new law, and the protests of Ipswich's citizenry were the most vocal and defiant of all. One August evening in 1687, the night before the town meeting, prominent men gathered at the home of John Appleton Jr., selectman and town clerk. John Andrews and Robert Kinsman, both selectmen, attended as did town constable Thomas French, Chebacco church deacon William Goodhue Jr., the Reverend William Hubbard of First Church, and the Reverend John Wise of the Chebacco parish. In all there were a dozen men in attendance who discussed the prevailing opinion against the tax law and devised a plan of action. The next day, the group proposed and the town agreed—in a unanimous vote—to demonstrate their displeasure by refusing to elect a tax commissioner.

The record of the meeting stated their case clearly: "Considering that the said act doth infringe their liberty as free born English subjects of his Majesty by interfering with the statutory laws of the land, by which it is enacted, that no taxes shall be levied on the subjects without consent of an assembly chosen by the freeholders for assessing the same."

The Ipswich leaders went a step further, sending representatives, including William Howlett, to influence the Rowley and Topsfield town meetings to follow suit. Haverhill and Andover also refused to elect tax commissioners.

The response was severe. Members of the Governor's Council—eight royalists appointed by Andros—sat as magistrates in the Ipswich court and began to call before them representatives of noncompliant towns. They also seized Ipswich's town book, containing the record of the town meeting. Ironically, it was turned over to Capt. John Appleton, a loyalist and the father of the town clerk. A long list of men from Essex County, including some from Ipswich, were called before the court. Most were released on bail. Particular offenders were singled out for harsher treatment, starting with John Appleton Jr., John Andrews, and Thomas French. A warrant for their arrest was issued on September 15, followed a day later with a warrant for the arrests of the Reverend John Wise and William Howlett. The five were held in Boston jail until their appearance several days later before Governor-General Andros and his council.

The arrests and jailings created a wave of panic and regret among a number of other recalcitrant officials in Essex County. They hurried to make amends to Andros before they, too, were committed to the stone jail in Boston Town.

On September 21, the Ipswich men along with various town officers from Salisbury, Bradford, and Rowley were arraigned before the council. The council declared that they were to be held until their trial for their refusal to pay taxes and for their seditious behavior, but the arraignment didn't go as smoothly as that. Wise protested that their privileges as Englishmen were being violated by the new tax law, to which one of the councilors replied, "Mr. Wise, you have no more privileges left you than not to be sold for slaves."

Francis Wainwright, another Ipswich resident who was present in the court that day, made the mistake of repeating this exchange and other negative comments made by the Andros council outside of the courtroom. This, of course, resulted in the council's displeasure and, fearing that he too might be tossed into jail, Wainwright apologized for his loose tongue in a "Humble Petition" to Andros and the council.

The band of jailed Ipswich leaders began to make humble petitions of their own seeking release on bail. These were refused by Andros. It would make a more powerful story to say that they stood steadfast during their imprisonment, but that wasn't the case. On September 28, the Ipswich delegation sent an even humbler communication to the governor-general pledging "willing subjection and dutiful observance." They further vowed to "endeavor a speedy prosecution and effecting of the work and service therein required in the making a list and assessment of the persons and estate of our town and transmit the same unto the treasurer."

Even this did not appease Andros, and the men remained in prison until their trial in October. The trial itself was little more than a formality. All the men pleaded not guilty to the charges of contempt and high misdemeanor. Little solid evidence was presented, but the jury—instructed well by Andros—convicted them all. Andros ordered them back to their cells to await sentencing three weeks later. Each of them received a heavy fine, was restricted from holding public office, and was required to put up £1,000 as a bond of good behavior.

Wise was banned from preaching, but that prohibition was lifted a month later after several influential people petitioned on his behalf. It is not clear, however, that the petition was truly what brought about the pardon. (A deal may have been arranged.) The day the ban was lifted was the same day that Ipswich submitted the town's tax money to Andros's treasurer.

However discomfited the Ipswich objectors may have been in the dank cells of Boston jail, their humiliation might have been assuaged a bit when they heard what befell Sir Edmund Andros two short years later, in 1689. After King James II, who had sent Andros to Massachusetts, was deposed, eager Bostonians seized Andros and many of his men. The night he was taken into custody Andros attempted an escape dressed in women's clothing, but he had neglected to change his shoes and was discovered. He spent nearly a year imprisoned in Boston before he was extradited to England.

While the Ipswich protest proved unsuccessful, the outcry against taxation without representation had been sounded. That vote of the Ipswich town meeting was a call for justice that would echo in the Revolution ninety years later.

The town seal honors this act of protest as a vital piece of Ipswich history. It bears the motto, "The Birthplace of American Independence, 1687." The event is also commemorated in a mural in the Ipswich post office.

WITCHES IN IPSWICH

The Puritans of the North Shore didn't take lightly accusations of familiarity with the devil and other dark acts.

In 1646, when one of the Pittford brothers claimed to have seen Jane James in a boat "in the likeness of a cat" and also said that his garden didn't produce well when he lived near her, James brought and won a slander suit against the Pittfords. Four years later, in 1650, they were at it again; this time James's husband received fifty shillings in damages for defamation of character (the Pittford brothers apparently were wont to run off their mouths, because several other people brought defamation suits against them). But rumors died hard, and in 1651 Jane James's husband was in court again, suing John Gatchell for calling his wife "an old witch" and telling tales that he saw her in a boat headed to Boston when she was also at home in her yard. Once again in 1667, James, by then a widow, won another suit against Richard Rowland, who claimed she had come in through his window and choked him.

These suits were typical of early witchcraft cases, where the charges were often slander and the accusers the ones punished. When Edmond Marshall was found guilty of slander for calling three women witches in 1653, his house and land were attached for damages, and within two weeks' time he had to appear before the meetinghouses in Ipswich, Salem, and Gloucester to acknowledge his wrongdoing.

This sensible approach to charges of witchcraft disappeared in 1692 with the sudden epidemic of accusations from the now-infamous group of girls in Salem Village.

Many of Salem's accused had their roots—and friends—in Ipswich. John Proctor and his wife Elizabeth were former residents of Chebacco. After their arrests, thirty-two of their Chebacco neighbors, led by the Reverend John Wise, signed a petition on their behalf. They attested that "as to what we have ever seen or heard of them upon our consciences we judge them innocent of the crime objected." Sarah Buckley, another former Ipswich resident, also received support when Ipswich's minister, the Reverend William Hubbard, wrote in her defense: "I have known Sarah, the wife of William Buckley of Salem Village, more or less ever since she was brought out of England which is above fifty years ago and during all that time I never knew nor heard of any evil in her carriage or conversation." The Proctors were condemned in August, and John was hanged; Elizabeth's execution was stayed because she was pregnant. Sarah Buckley was acquitted at her trial in 1693.

Mehitabel Brabrooke Downing, the same servant girl who had burned down the Perkins house years before, now a grown woman and a wife, was accused and arrested in May. She was imprisoned for about a year. Elizabeth Howe, who cared for her blind husband and managed their farm on the Ipswich-Topsfield line, was arrested in May, tried in June, and hanged in July.

By the end of September over 150 accused witches languished in the jails of Ipswich, Salem, Boston, and Cambridge; to ease the crowding some of the prisoners were contracted out to local residents who were paid by the colonial government for their upkeep. Those held at the Ipswich jail included Sarah Good and her tiny daughter Dorcas, Sarah Wildes, Ann Pudeator, Martha and Giles Corey (who made out his will while jailed in Ipswich), and Mary Easty, the sister of Rebecca Nurse. Jailkeeper Thomas Fossie and his wife both testified on Goodwife Easty's behalf, but to no avail. All but young Dorcas Good were eventually put to death.

In October, with a total of twenty victims executed, the governor disbanded the Court of Oyer and Terminer, which had been established in May solely for these witchcraft trials. A superior court tried the remaining cases. The last trials took place in Ipswich on May 9, 1693. None of these resulted in a guilty verdict, and the remaining accused were ordered released from jail.

Despite their support for certain individuals, the people of Ipswich played their own shameful part in the witchcraft drama of 1692. On the heels of the first wave of accusations in Salem, several Ipswich residents accused Rachel Clinton of being a witch. She had come to Ipswich in the 1630s as the young daughter of a wealthy man and sixty years later was a divorced, lonely old woman living in poverty and dependent on the town. Perhaps some hard-hearted residents may have viewed the wave of witch arrests as an opportunity to be rid of a drain on the public coffers. On March 29 she was accused, arrested, and taken to Ipswich court. A similar charge had been made against her in 1687 when her neighbors, the Fullers, testified against her. They spoke up again, citing Goody Clinton's connection to the death of Betty Fuller. The fact that Betty had actually recovered from her illness and wasn't dead at all perhaps didn't come up in court. The sixty-three-year-old woman was imprisoned for nearly a year; she died in Ipswich in 1695.

EIGHTEENTH CENTURY

IPSWICH IN THE EIGHTEENTH CENTURY

In the 1700s Ipswich was shaped by evolution and revolution. As the century opened, the colonial seaport bustled with successful fishing and shipping industries, shipbuilding in Chebacco flourished, and farming in the Hamlet prospered. A hundred years later Ipswich was part of a new nation, but it was also in economic decline. The one town became three: The Hamlet was incorporated as Hamilton, and Chebacco became Essex not long after the nineteenth century's turn.

OH, FOR THE REST OF THE STORY!

An all-too-brief item in the *New England Journal* reports an incident from October 1727: "We are informed, from Ipswich, that on Wednesday night last, a young woman of that place, being more merry than wise, dressed herself in men's apparel, intending a frolic at a place some distance off; but as she was riding through a river or pond, her horse, in all likelihood, threw her into the water, where she was taken up the next day drowned."

Who this young woman was, why she was abroad dressed in borrowed breeches, and what unwise merrymaking she had planned we'll never know.

❖

SPIRITUAL SHAKE-UP

The year 1727 was a difficult one, and a strange one for weather. A drought dragged on from June to September, and great heat during July added to the misery. The sky was frequently disturbed by lightning but there was no rain. When the drought finally broke, it was no gentle rainfall; a fierce nor'easter brought wind, rain, and destructively high tides that washed away haystacks from the marshes and pounded boats upon the shore. Barely a month later, mid-October was bitter cold. Snow fell. The twenty-ninth was a pleasant contrast to the days before—fair and mild. Late that evening, despite a clear sky, a rumble like thunder arose, growing louder and more frightening as though thousands of riders on horseback were galloping at breakneck speed into the villages. The thundering was followed by a mere minute of the earthquake's shock itself, but what a minute it must have been in the dark of night to frightened families! Several aftershocks followed the original quake, and many people spent a sleepless night.

Disconcerted residents viewed the earthquake as a spiritual wake-up call. Ministers claimed it was an act of God to call attention to a slackening in their religious observance. Penitence trembled through the citizenry like an aftershock. Ninety-four new names were recorded in the church membership of Chebacco parish following the earthquake. Ninety-nine were inspired to join the ranks of the faithful in the Hamlet parish.

Another earthquake struck on a Sunday morning, June 3, 1744, during the sermon of the Reverend Mr. Wigglesworth in the Hamlet (what would later become the town of Hamilton). The rumbling quake rattled the meetinghouse windows and doors. Without skipping a beat, the cool-headed minister said to his nervous congregation, "There can be no better place for us to die in than the house of God."

❖

THE CHOATES OF THE ISLAND

John Choate, an early settler of Ipswich, gave land to his three elder sons and a Harvard education to the youngest. His son Thomas received as his acreage Hog Island, which sat in the waters between Ipswich proper and Chebacco. Thomas built a house, established a farm, and started raising generations of island-born Choates.

His domain earned Thomas the nickname "Governor Choate," and over the years the island, commonly referred to as Choate Island, often seemed like a colony unto itself as its multigenerational population grew. The "Governor" left his province in 1725 for a house on the mainland, and after the earthquake of 1727 he decided to divide his land holdings among his own sons; the island went to his son Francis, who in turn left it to his son William.

By the late 1700s the island bustled with the activities of several farms, a small school, the comings and goings of sons who were seamen, and the inevitable attentions of mainland boys toward the growing selection of young and available Choate women. William had five daughters himself, and there were eleven more female cousins of marriageable age all on the island at one time. One stalwart mainlander made an expedition to Choate Island in search of a bride and presented himself to Mary Choate, William's wife, declaring, "I have come courting. Which girl shall I take?" The expedition was a success, and more mainland boys followed.

The island was home to succeeding generations of Choates, though in time they occupied it mainly in the summer months. In 1916 the Choate family sold the island to Richard T. Crane Jr., a wealthy Chicago industrialist who had already purchased considerable property on Castle Neck. In 1975 the Crane family donated the island to the Trustees of Reservations. Francis Choate's eighteenth-century house still stands on the island.

❖

Turn out for the boat launching

Boat launches in Chebacco were social events. Everyone turned out to help and to share in the pleasure of a job brought to fruition. It didn't matter whether a shipwright built his boat in the yards by the river or nearer his home, perhaps a mile or more away from the water—not when there were neighbors willing to help with a launching.

On launching day men brought teams of oxen, and the boat-builder supplied the rum. The men raised up the newly constructed boat on several sets of oversized wooden wheels, and the ox teams pulled it to a spot on the river bank. There the wheels could roll right down into the water until the boat floated—a moment undoubtedly accompanied by great cheering and a final toast or two.

The contest was the very personification of the minister's words,
the struggle of man against Satan.

❖

A DEVIL OF A TIME IN IPSWICH

A favorite Ipswich legend concerns Satan himself and a celebrity of the eighteenth century. A "Great Awakening" of religious fervor swept through the American colonies midway through the eighteenth century, and the Reverend George Whitefield of England was a major leader of the revival. He traveled throughout the colonies in the 1740s, drawing vast crowds with his dynamic sermons and powerful delivery while raising money for an orphanage he hoped to build in the new colony of Georgia. His message stirred highly emotional responses in many of his listeners and inspired their fervent rededication to their religion. It must be said that not all members of the clergy approved of Whitefield's emotionalism, and the wave of revivalism created conflict in the churches.

No less a critic than Benjamin Franklin wrote of Whitefield's prowess as an orator. "He had a loud and clear voice, and articulated his words and sentences so perfectly that he might be heard and understood at a great distance," Franklin noted in his autobiography. Scientist that he was, Franklin went so far as to calculate how many listeners stood in one of Whitefield's huge outdoor audiences in the streets of Philadelphia. Allowing for two square feet per person, Franklin computed that the gathering numbered thirty thousand people, an estimate he was happy to find confirmed by the local newspaper.

The Reverend Mr. Whitefield was a savvy showman. He often scheduled multiple appearances at each stop on his tour to reinforce his message through repetition and allow his audiences to grow by word of mouth. In the fall of 1740, he made his first visit to the Boston area, scheduling a week of appearances through towns to the north. His ambitious itinerary usually included two sermons a day in two different towns.

According to his journals, Whitefield first preached in Ipswich on Tuesday, September 30, at ten o'clock in the morning to a crowd of thousands. His preaching apparently had great effect on the listeners, even by his own estimation. "There was a great melting in the congregation," he wrote in his journal of that first Ipswich sermon.

His tour, which went as far north as York, Maine, brought him back to Ipswich on Saturday, October 4, when he delivered another morning sermon at First Church on Meetinghouse Hill to an even larger congregation. It was during this oratory, according to legend, that the devil came to Ipswich to hear Whitefield and the uncomplimentary things the powerful preacher was saying about him.

The two squared off, wrestling on the floor of the church to the astonishment of onlookers. So involved were the combatants that they continued the fight to the very top of the steeple. The contest was the very personification of the minister's words, the struggle of man against Satan, with man seeming to gain the upper hand one moment and the devil nearly overpowering him the next. In the end, good triumphed over evil, as the devil either leapt or was thrown (depending on the version of the legend) from the steeple heights. He landed feet first, causing a flash of sparks on the outcropping below, and the spot is forever marked by his footprint in the rock.

Unfortunately for history, Whitefield's only journal notation about this second sermon in Ipswich lacks juicy details. It reads, "Collected £79 for the orphans." Perhaps taking on the devil face-to-face and hand-to-hand was commonplace for Whitefield and not at all noteworthy.

❖

The man and his bridge

One of the most recognizable landmarks in Ipswich is the stone arch bridge that spans the Ipswich River near the center of town. Early in the town's history, small wooden footbridges had sufficed when traffic was light and transport was generally on foot or on horseback. But with the coming of the first stage route through Ipswich in 1762 (a weekly run between Portsmouth and Boston), as well as the acquisition by some of chaises and sleighs, people began to worry about the old wooden bridge under its heavier loads.

A four-man committee was appointed in 1764 to oversee the improvement of the bridge, the cost to be divided evenly between the town and the county. The committee consisted of Joseph Appleton, Aaron Potter, Capt. Isaac Smith, and Col. John Choate. Choate pushed for replacement instead of improvement and proposed constructing the new bridge of stone. His fellow committee members, like others in town, were less than enthusiastic about the idea, doubting that the riverbanks could support the weight of such a structure. Colonel Choate must have been a persuasive man, however, because construction began that June. Choate took a leave of absence from the General Court to oversee the project. He donated his time to the effort as did Appleton and Smith, while Potter was paid twenty pounds for keeping the accounts and measuring rocks.

What is generally acknowledged to be the first stone-arch bridge in English-speaking North America took five months to build. The stones were unfinished granite, the same common rocks used to construct the area's ubiquitous stone walls. Each was laid carefully into place. Wooden scaffolds supported the two arches as the bridge took shape. The total cost of the project was just under £1,000.

A crowd gathered under a bright October sky to observe the opening ceremony. Colonel Choate, on horseback, stood at the north end of the bridge with his nephew Stephen while a blind man from Rowley recited a poem that he had written to commemorate the occasion. The onlookers collectively held their breath as Choate gave the order to remove the supports from beneath the arches. The stone marvel stood!

Cynics said that Choate had awaited the first test of the bridge's soundness on the north side of the river so that he would be in good position to flee to Canada if the bridge collapsed, but all had to admit that his brainchild was a success.

Choate often succeeded when circumstances seemed to dictate failure. He was a lawyer and longtime public servant—representative to the General Court, member of the Executive Council, and justice and chief justice in the Court of Sessions and Court of Common Pleas—despite the fact that he wasn't particularly good at reading or writing. This shortcoming did not go unnoticed in the Massachusetts House of Representatives where, on one occasion, Choate submitted a report to the Speaker, who, after frowning over it for a time, declared the handwriting unreadable and announced that there wasn't a single word spelled correctly in the entire document. Choate, who apparently lacked nothing in oral communication skills, quick thinking, or sense of humor, pointed out to the Speaker that his report contained the word *the*, correctly spelled *t-h-e*.

NATHANIEL ROGERS, ETCHED IN STONE

A walk through the old burying ground on High Street offers visitors a fascinating glimpse at the town's history in shorthand, carved on gravestones in messages tantalizingly brief and not always decipherable.

One stone is a decided contrast to its terse neighbors. It marks the grave of the Reverend Nathaniel Rogers who died in 1775. It is tall (five feet) and broad and so well carved that it is easily readable over two hundred years later.

A visitor can learn much about the life of Nathaniel Rogers from a gravestone that is biographical sketch, eulogy, and portrait all in one. The twenty-five lines of text get smaller in size and closer together toward the bottom, as though the carver was running out of room (and didn't have the luxury of simply turning the page). The faithful friend or family member who wrote the text obviously felt the great responsibility of capturing the illustrious man's life and influence.

Although the stone-carved story is extensive, it doesn't tell all. Nathaniel Rogers followed in his father's footsteps as the pastor of the First Church. The younger Rogers was ordained in Ipswich in 1727 (the lavish gathering to celebrate the occasion included beef, pork, mutton, and chicken as well as nineteen gallons of wine). He served as an assistant minister to his father, John, for eighteen years before taking over as head pastor. Nathaniel Rogers's service to First Church lasted nearly fifty years "until death translated him to the high reward of his labors," according to the epitaph. His tenure coincided with major changes in the religious life of Ipswich: The revival spirit of the Great Awakening in the 1740s heralded a period of tumultuous growth in which three new churches appeared—South Parish (split off from First Church), Fourth Church (created by a division of the Chebacco Church), and Linebrook Church (with parishioners who lived along the Ipswich-Rowley line). Rogers also oversaw the construction of a new meetinghouse for his own First Parish.

Two subsequent meetinghouses have risen on that same site, and South Parish and First Parish have reunited since Rogers's time. In one way, Nathaniel Rogers has stayed to see it all: Above the adoring lines on the gravestone is an image of the man himself, a portrait in relief. The carver was a stickler for detail. The portrait captures the lines and curls of Rogers's shoulder-length wig, the folds of his robe, and the points of his collar. His waistcoat even boasts fourteen buttons, with fourteen buttonholes.

EVERY WISE WOMAN

The women and girls of Ipswich took part in the Revolutionary War in their own way. Cloth was in short supply during the war and the years preceding it due to the trade restrictions and import taxes imposed by the royal government. To ease the shortages the

*Not everyone was caught up in the hysteria of
the Great Ipswich Fright.*

industrious women gathered for spinning bees. The gatherings were social as well as socially responsible. Often held at the home of the minister, the bees generally included a spiritually inspiring lecture to entertain the women while they worked.

One such bee, held on a June day in 1769, took place at the home of the Reverend John Cleaveland. Seventy-seven women, ages thirteen and up, carded and spun until six o'clock in the evening. In one day they produced 440 knots of linen yarn, 730 knots of cotton, and 600 knots of tow (a fiber made from flax, hemp, or jute).

While they labored, Cleaveland entertained them with a sermon, basing his remarks on a verse from Proverbs: "Every wise woman buildeth her house: but the foolish plucketh it down with her hands." He also encouraged their efforts to live on locally produced goods and their commitment to boycott the "pernicious weed," as tea was known around town in those days.

❖

THE GREAT IPSWICH FRIGHT

Several weeks after the battles at Lexington and Concord (which took place on Wednesday, April 19, 1775), Ipswich voted to continue posting four men on the town watch. Two were stationed on Castle Hill, where they kept an eye out for British invaders coming by sea to steal sheep and cattle from the common grazing lands. A beacon was erected on the hill and a supply of tar (fuel for the beacon) was laid in, so the watch could signal invasion by night. A flag would signal the alarm by day.

These measures were probably a response to the false alarm that had panicked the town on Thursday, April 20. Nearly three hundred Ipswich minutemen had left town on the previous afternoon to answer the summons to battle, so the remaining townsfolk were already in a nervous state. The call to arms had reached as far north as Hampton, New Hampshire, and that town's company traveled all night, marching into Ipswich on Thursday morning to find the residents in a frenzy. Capt. Jonathan Burnham, head of the Hampton company, was told by frantic Ipswich folk that two British warships were lying in the river. British troops, they said, were about to land, first to free redcoats held in the jail and then to burn the town.

Apparently, no one thought to verify that there were indeed warships in the river before spreading the alarm. By Friday, messengers had spread the wild rumor up the coast, creating a tidal wave of panic. Ipswich residents fled north on the heels of their Rowley neighbors. Salisbury citizens evacuated to Hampton, where they stayed in the empty houses of those who had retreated even farther north. Men and women rushed about hiding their valuables and packing what they could for a hasty exodus.

Not everyone was caught up in the hysteria. Eliphalet Hale, a visitor from Exeter, New Hampshire, lingered in Ipswich to find out the truth of the situation. Once he realized that the alarm was false, he rode through the countryside spreading the news and trying to quell the madness. Unlike the riders on the eve of the confrontations at Lexington and Concord, Hale's cry was that the British *were not* coming.

Elizabeth Ringe, a dedicated Ipswich woman, went about her usual washing-day routine. When her father (who had just finished burying his silverware in his cellar) came to her house to help her prepare for the evacuation, he was startled to find her calmly scrubbing a kettle full of clothing. He tried excitedly to rouse her to action, but she replied coolly that if the British were coming to ransack her home, they could just as well have the clothes wet as dry.

❖

FIRST TO FALL

Of Saturday, June 17, 1775, the Reverend Manasseh Cutler, at the Hamlet, noted in his journal: "Studied. Heard that there was an engagement at Charlestown. In the afternoon saw a very great smoke, and at night saw the light of the fire which was the burning of Charlestown by the Regular forces. At the same time there was a very smart engagement at the small breastwork raised by our people on Bunker's Hill. . . . It was supposed that there were 5,000 Regulars, and not more than 2,000 or 3,000 of our men that actually engaged in the fight. Our loss is supposed to be about 50 killed and 20 or 30 taken prisoner."

Among the dead at the Battle of Bunker Hill was Jesse Story of Chebacco, the first Ipswich soldier to fall in the war. Young Story, just eighteen years old, was one of forty men who enlisted in Capt. Abraham Dodge's company from Chebacco. After early success in thwarting the advance of the British regulars, the Continentals ran low on ammunition; they knew they would have to retreat because so few of them were equipped with the bayonets they would need when the redcoats reached their lines. Sure enough, a contingent of British soldiers managed to maneuver around to another slope of the hill, attacking the Continentals' fortification from the other side with a swell of bright uniforms, snapping guns, and roaring cannons. Surrounded by smoke and noise and the confusion of the fight, Jesse Story had only moments to live.

Another of the company, Francis Burnham, was an eyewitness to the tragedy: "We were now attacked on both sides, and the contest became very hot. Story and I were side by side, when a ball struck his head, his brains flew into my face and he fell back into the ditch, which ran along behind the fence. Another shot gave me a slight wound upon the shoulder, which made me stop for a few moments to get breath."

The confrontation with the well-equipped British troops must have seemed daunting to Story, Burnham, and their comrades who went into battle with only the clothes and arms they brought from home. Another Ipswich soldier recalled the battle and the British forces: "When they got so near we could fairly see them, they looked too handsome to be fired at, but we had to do it."

Jesse Story's father had to make a list of his son's possessions in order to be reimbursed for the lost items: one gun, one bayonet, one pound of powder, one dozen flints, thirty balls, one knapsack, two jackets, one pair of breeches, one shirt, stockings, shoes, and a hat. Most of these were lost in the battle, but when the army sent Jesse's body home to his family, they sent along one other item—the cannonball that killed him.

MAKING DO

Wartime shortages of many imported goods forced the folk of Ipswich to devise creative uses for materials at hand. One commodity that was sorely missed was molasses, which had been imported from the West Indies. But although sugar cane was absent from Ipswich's fields, corn grew in abundance, and the Reverend Manasseh Cutler, who was a knowledgeable botanist and inquisitive scientist, decided to experiment with cornstalks in place of cane. He ground the cornstalks, reserved the liquid, and boiled it down to the consistency of molasses. The result had a bit more of a bite than sugar cane molasses, but in time of war it was sweeter than no molasses at all. Baked in a pudding it had as fine a taste as any treat.

If molasses from sugar cane could be distilled into rum, Cutler decided a few days later that he just had to find out if his corn-based concoction could serve as well. Certainly it was scientific curiosity that enticed him to distill his newfangled molasses; his journal notes simply, "Boiled cornstalk liquor." As with his earlier efforts, this endeavor also met with positive results, and we can surmise that his friends and neighbors toasted his ingenuity.

THE CLEAVELANDS TO ARMS

The Reverend John Cleaveland was an enthusiastic supporter of the fight for liberty. As the outspoken minister of the Chebacco parish, Cleaveland had been an influential presence in the village for thirty years. It must have come as little surprise when, with war on the horizon, he exhorted the young men of the village—including his four sons—to take up the cause of liberty.

The senior Cleaveland served in the Revolution as a chaplain, as he had in the French and Indian War. He may have been eager to answer the call to arms again as it gave him the opportunity to get away from the day-to-day strains of raising a large family on a minister's small salary. Because of his financial limitations, Cleaveland had been unable to send any of his sons to college, a hard reality for the ambitious father. His eldest son, John Jr., had moved to Canterbury, Connecticut (John Sr.'s hometown); there he married a cousin and took up work on her family's farm. The second son, Parker, studied medicine for two years and settled with his new wife in Byfield. The younger boys, Ebenezer and Nehemiah, were among the children still living at home in 1775.

The menfolk of the Cleaveland family were reunited in Cambridge, where colonists were laying siege to British-occupied Boston. John Jr., a restless and unhappy young man, found satisfaction in his military service and was promoted from sergeant to lieutenant during his tour of duty. After the war he returned to Chebacco and studied with his father for the ministry. He was ordained in 1785.

For Parker, the army was little more than a new arena for his father to press his ambitions for his son. Cleaveland persuaded Dr. Joseph Warren, the acting surgeon general, to post Parker as a surgeon in the sixteenth regiment, but a short time later Parker was replaced. Cleaveland was livid, but he could do nothing about it. Parker returned home and spent most of the war years in his private practice.

Nehemiah, the youngest son, served as an aide to his father in Cambridge and again on Long Island in 1776. In 1780, at the age of nineteen, Nehemiah joined the Continental army as a private and served a six-month tour of duty in an artillery company. After the war he followed his brother Parker into the field of medicine.

Son Ebenezer had the most unfortunate time, both in his young life and during the war years. A childhood accident cost him an eye and scarred his face, but he overcame this handicap. Trained as a cooper before the war, he left his trade to serve as an assistant to his brother Parker in the sixteenth regiment and later as a seaman on a privateer. Between assignments Ebenezer returned home, married, and moved to the village of Little Cambridge (now Belmont). The couple had a son that died in infancy, but soon after, Ebenezer and Mary had another son. In 1779, Ebenezer signed on with a merchant ship bound for the West Indies, hoping the change in climate would improve his deteriorating health. When the ship was boarded by a British privateer; Ebenezer was mistakenly identified as a deserter from the Royal Navy and taken prisoner. He managed to escape once the British ship reached the West Indies. There he signed on with a Dutch ship, which was itself apprehended by the French for transporting contraband and its entire crew thrown into prison in Guadeloupe. This series of hardships did little to improve the young man's health, but unlike many of his shipmates, he survived imprisonment. Rescued by a Continental privateer, Ebenezer was working as a seaman and bound home for New England when he succumbed to the "prison fever" that had taken so many in Guadeloupe. He died on March 30, 1780.

As for the family patriarch, war's end restored his life to its pre-war condition, which included a crowded household (Ebenezer's widow and son lived there for a while) and a minister's meager salary.

❖

LIGHTNING STRIKES TWICE IN THE HAMLET

In March 1781, Samuel Adams sat with his family in their home in the Hamlet while the thunderstorm roared outside. His wife moved about the fire readying their meal. His daughter rose from her seat on the hearth and stretched, smiling at the dog that immediately curled up in the warm spot she had vacated. Suddenly a bolt of lightning flashed down the chimney and struck one of the andirons. The shock knocked Mrs. Adams to the floor unconscious and killed the dog instantly.

Adams may have thought of his family's close call ten years later when he and his two sons were caught in a June storm. They spotted a large oak tree that seemed a likely shelter and ran toward it as the rain increased. Their dog bounded ahead of them, enjoying the race, and reached the tree just as lightning struck. This dog, too, was killed instantly. One of the sons was knocked unconscious, but like his mother before him, he was revived unharmed.

PEACE

When word reached Ipswich in early spring of 1783 that peace had been declared, the town wasted little time in planning a celebration. On April 29, everyone turned out to rejoice. At ten o'clock crowds filled First Church to hear a reading of the peace proclamation from Congress and an oration by the Reverend Levi Frisbie. A prayer and several hymns were followed by the firing of thirteen cannons, and the town gathered on the green for a celebratory meal. Long tables were covered with meats and food and spirits; it seemed that everyone had contributed to the feast, and everyone enjoyed it. Thirteen toasts were made and the thirteen cannons fired again and again. If that was not enough to make revelers' ears ring, a grand fireworks display exploded in the skies over town that evening. To add to the spectacle, many people illuminated their houses. The dark days of war were finally over.

GREETINGS TO LAFAYETTE

As a hero of the Revolutionary War, the Marquis de Lafayette received a warm welcome from Americans when he toured the young United States in 1784. On a visit to Ipswich, Lafayette was

Gen. Michael Farley, a highly respected man of Ipswich, intended to greet the Marquis de Lafayette by removing his hat as he bowed, but he accidentally removed his wig as well.

met by Gen. Michael Farley, a tanner in peacetime and a representative to the General Court and delegate to the Provincial Congress in the difficult years preceding the war. Farley, a highly respected man of Ipswich, intended to greet the great man by removing his hat as he bowed, but he accidentally removed his wig as well. Several other members of the welcoming party—either out of respect for Farley or because they thought he knew some odd bit of French etiquette of which they were unaware—doffed their wigs along with their hats as well.

UNEXPECTED JOURNEY

Wednesday, December 6, 1786, found Maj. Charles Smith with his two sons looking for sheep that had strayed during a snowstorm that had raged for the past two days. As they trudged across the open land of Great Neck, a blanket of new snow sparkled in the bright sun with the same diamond brightness that bounced off the waters of the nearby bay. The sound of a voice calling reached their ears, and they looked across the narrow stretch of water to Little Neck.

The shore was strewn with ruined haystacks washed down from the marshes during the storm, and upon one of these stood a man waving his arms and calling to them. Major Smith waded across the shallowest part of the waterway. When he reached the shore, he found not one but two men, Samuel Elwell and Samuel Pulsifer of Rowley, with an unusual tale to tell.

They had started out Monday morning to go clamming on the flats in Plum Island Sound. The two men had a small hut on one of the islands near the Rowley marshes where they planned to spend the night, but the storm came up at midday on Monday and they decided to return home. With low tide upon them they started across the marshes. They trudged among the many graying humps of marsh hay stacked on wooden staddles and slipped on the chunks of ice heaved up along the creeks. As the snow grew

Elwell and Pulsifer were adrift on a most unlikely craft.

heavier, it became harder to see. They became disoriented and soon had to admit to being lost.

Finally the two took shelter in one of the many haystacks around them, burrowing into its bristly center to wait out the storm. Night passed. The storm blew on, and the tide rose quickly. They scrambled to the top of the haystack and saw around them other haystacks already rising from their staddles and floating away. They wondered how high the tide would rise and if their weight would be enough to keep their own nest of hay firmly on its framing. They worried. They waited.

Catastrophe struck in the form of a large cake of ice floating on the high waters which collided with the haystack and knocked it off the staddle. Elwell and Pulsifer were adrift on a most unlikely craft. The haystack floated at the mercy of the wind and currents, spinning and bobbing or racing along, as the men clung to their perch and prayed that the stack would not break apart suddenly and plunge them into the icy water. The storm-blown waves pulled at the haystack hour after hour, and it did begin to come apart, so when another haystack crashed into the one they were riding, Elwell and Pulsifer made a quick switch. They watched the first stack scatter like so many straws in the swirling waters.

The hours in the cold wind and snow took their toll on the two men, who were soaked to the bone. Exposure made them groggy, and they struggled to keep awake and keep their seats. Finally, the wind blew them close to land, which they could see beyond a ragged border of ice. The two men eyed the firm ground wearily. The raft-sized ice cakes strewn haphazardly along the shore seemed too great an obstacle for them to overcome.

Slowly Pulsifer realized that the haystack was drifting away, and rising panic spurred him into action. He jumped onto the ice and yelled for his friend to follow. Elwell was nearly overcome with the cold, but he caught on to one of the rafts of ice and floated to shore. Pulsifer waded in, struggling to move his legs at all.

On dry land, the men ran about to restore their circulation and clear their heads. Then they found a dry haystack and burrowed in for warmth and rest. Once refreshed, they took stock of their surroundings: an island, deserted, yet in clear view of the nearby mainland. The storm had ended and the day was bright and clear. Elwell and Pulsifer climbed to the top of the hill; Pulsifer spotted a figure on the mainland, and the two called out as loudly as they could, but the man didn't hear them and presently disappeared from sight. Cold and hungry, the men began to lose hope. They returned to their haystack and flopped down in discouragement.

But it was less than an hour later when they looked across the bright water and spotted a man and two boys striding along on the mainland. Pulsifer leaped to the top of the haystack, waving his arms and calling.

❖

Manasseh Cutler

The Reverend Manasseh Cutler was a man of many interests and just as many talents. The minister of the Hamlet church also served as a physician to supplement his income during the Revolutionary War. As a director of the Ohio Company, he helped negotiate with Congress the terms of the ordinance for the governance of the Ohio Territory, which included strong provisions for education and the exclusion of slavery. Back home he was also an important figure in negotiations to separate the Hamlet from Ipswich and incorporate the former as the town of Hamilton.

He was an avid natural scientist, with an interest in astronomy, meteorology, geology, and, most especially, botany. Cutler was a keen observer with a curious mind. His journal contains descriptions of a vast array of things in the world around him—a comparison of hair and fur as viewed through a microscope, the aurora borealis, comet sightings, the effects of earthquakes, the workings of a steam engine, and great detail on the plants and trees in his garden.

Cutler was just as perceptive an observer of people. On his journey to Congress in 1787 regarding the Ohio Territory, he had the opportunity to meet Benjamin Franklin, whom he greatly admired. While he expected to meet some sort of American royalty in the learned scientist and statesman, what he encountered was "a short, fat, trunched old man, in a plain Quaker dress, bald pate, and short white socks, sitting without his hat under the tree." He was delighted when Franklin showed him a preserved two-headed snake, a glass machine that simulated blood circulation through the body, an early copy machine, and a huge book on botany that the two perused for several hours. He noted with admiration Franklin's energy (despite his age of eighty-four), his sense of humor, and his seemingly endless store of knowledge. Cutler also wrote that while Franklin's daughter seemed to have little or no control over her children, they were very fond of their grandfather.

His descriptions of people were detailed and direct whether he was well acquainted with them or encountered them only briefly. At a dinner in New York he sat with a marquis ("if it had not been for his title, I should have thought him two-thirds of a fool") and a woman with a most unusual hairstyle—he recalled with disgust the particulars of its construction, which even included wiring. At a rather rundown tavern in Connecticut he considered the innkeeper "a churlish clown," while he found the man's wife very pleasant and thought she deserved both a better house and a better husband. A visit with an acquaintance from his college days— the sister of one of his chums—inspired musings about "the baneful effects of time" on beautiful, young women. He noted, "She was certainly very pretty, but she is now extremely ugly." In context the remark seems forthright rather than mean, a candid scientific commentary, as it is followed shortly without even a paragraph break by another observation: "Weathersfield is a pleasant village."

Cutler was pastor in the Hamlet and Hamilton for fifty-three years until his death in 1823 at the age of eighty. He is buried in the Hamilton cemetery across the street from the church he served and the house where he lived. The Cutler Elementary School was named in his honor.

WASHINGTON PAUSED HERE

On October 30, 1789, all Ipswich was abuzz with great anticipation. President George Washington was traveling through the New England states—and stopping here. Citizens turned out in all of the many towns along his route, and Washington no doubt was honored at ceremonies at each stop, no matter how brief. The three hours he tarried in Ipswich were no exception.

The revered guest was met at the edge of town by the selectmen and escorted into Ipswich. A regiment assembled on the south green for his review, and afterwards he stood on the steps of Homan's Inn, flanked by Ipswich residents John Heard and Nathaniel Wade, as the crowds gathered to see and hear everything the great man did. A fortunate few were presented to the president, including Rebekah Dodge, who had turned six just a few weeks before. Her late father, Abraham, like Heard and Wade, had served Washington as an officer in the Revolutionary army. The little girl looked up at the new president, and he patted her on the head and gave her a kiss, much to the crowd's delight.

After the presentations and much waving and tipping of his hat, Washington repaired to the inn, stopping long enough for a cold drink and to meet several gentlemen from Newburyport who were to escort him to the next stop on his tour.

TREES AS A POLITICAL STATEMENT

In the 1790s Lombardy poplars were fashionable trees for planting along roadsides in Ipswich and many other areas. The tall, straight trees were introduced to the United States by Thomas Jefferson, who had seen them in France. The species had been brought to France from Asia fifty years earlier, but got its

European name from the Lombardy region where the trees often grew along riverbanks.

Not only did displaying the poplars show a European flair, it allowed local landowners to make a political statement: The trees were often planted by Jeffersonian Republicans as a demonstration of their support for Jefferson's ideas. Lombardy poplars became a target of criticism—and sometimes vandalism—by Federalists who disagreed with Republican views.

Political targets or not, the poplars were not suited to the New England climate. Their nearly vertical branches frequently died or decayed, and the trees were often broken or uprooted in storms. The unfortunate plantings hardly needed vandals to add to their misery. After it was discovered that the Lombardy poplars had a negative effect on the soil and were occasionally imported with poisonous snakes inhabiting their branches, they fell out of fashion. But by then, with or without political landscaping, Jefferson was in the White House.

❖

TIMES OF TROUBLE

In the early 1700s, fishing and shipping thrived hand-in-hand; Ipswich sea captains transported fish caught by Ipswich fishermen for trade in the West Indies, while shipbuilders in Ipswich proper and others in Chebacco provided vessels for their seagoing neighbors. But a series of wars interfered with maritime commerce, and the silting of the Ipswich River made its shallower waterway inaccessible to large vessels. By the end of the American Revolution, Ipswich was deep in debt and, like the rest of the new nation, in the throes of an economic depression. A British ban on the import of American fish to the British West Indies effectively destroyed this major market for local fishermen; a British decree that American goods could enter British ports only aboard British vessels damaged the shipping industry as well. When England and

France went to war in the 1790s, the British harassed American merchant ships bound for ports in the French West Indies, and American vessels were seized and sold. The United States tried to remain neutral, but as the prospect of another war with Britain loomed and the threat to American ships grew, President Thomas Jefferson declared an embargo in 1807.

To make matters worse the residents of both the Hamlet and Chebacco parishes had begun talking during the 1700s about separating from Ipswich and becoming towns in their own right. The biggest issue stirring the desire for independence was the support of the poor. Changing times and fortunes had made the old hub of the settlement less prosperous than the two offspring parishes. The Hamlet was a thriving farming community, and shipbuilding continued to drive the economy in Chebacco, which retained easy access to the ocean. Most of those dependent on public care lived in Ipswich proper.

In 1793, the Hamlet successfully petitioned the state government for incorporation as a separate town and became Hamilton; the act of separation required Hamilton to pay $950 to Ipswich toward support for the poor.

Ipswich's straits only worsened. The next year the town painted a bleak picture in a petition to the General Court: "This place has for many years past been on the decline. . . . The present inhabitants are obliged to support many poor persons who have passed many of their useful days and expended all their property in other towns, but having gained no legal settlement elsewhere return to us for maintenance and support—which increase of our expense has caused a valuable part lately to separate from us and thrown on us an additional burden."

From its first days, Ipswich, like other Puritan settlements, had considered it the town's duty to care for those unable to support themselves. The first poorhouse was constructed sometime in the 1600s, the second in 1717. By 1795, the town needed new accommodations. The town purchased the farm of John Harris, which was used for several years, but by 1817 Ipswich was in the market for another property. The ongoing expenditures frustrated the residents of Chebacco just as they had the people of the Hamlet. On New Year's Day 1818, the town voted an appropriation of $10,500 for the purchase of a new farm for the poor; as far as Chebacco was concerned, that was the last straw.

In April 1818, the state legislature received a petition from Chebacco parish requesting separation from Ipswich. A year later Chebacco became incorporated as the town of Essex (paying Ipswich $3,000 for its share of town debts).

Ipswich sold the old Harris property, using the proceeds of the sale to make improvements on the new poor farm.

PILLOW LACE

Even though wearing lace had been the subject of legal proceedings in the late 1600s, in the 1700s lace making became a skill that the women of Ipswich passed on to their daughters. By the end of the century, it developed into a prosperous cottage industry. Women and girls tatted both white and black lacework of cotton, silk, and linen thread on lap pillows. They formed patterns by sticking straight pins into these firm bolsters, corresponding to points of a diagram poked into a piece of parchment or pasteboard. The pillows were personal items, sized and shaped to fit the lap of their owners, who often tucked notes, snacks, or other small articles inside their pillow's lining for safekeeping.

Most of the women's equipment, like the lace itself, was homemade. They used materials they had on hand or that grew nearby. The pillows were homespun cloth stuffed with marsh grass which was then covered with fabric from old dresses or stockings. The bobbins were cut from reeds that grew in the marshes. Only the pins and the thread needed to be imported.

When families faced economic hardship, lace was a useful form of currency; women sometimes traded their handiwork for goods from local merchants. Often the women sold their lace out of town; one woman, the lace merchant, took all of the output of a group of Ipswich lace makers to sell in Boston or as far away as Maine, then returned with the proceeds for each of the women.

In one year, between August 1789 and August 1790, approximately forty-two thousand yards of lace were produced in Ipswich by some six hundred lace makers. That's seventy yards per woman, worked in fine thread with tiny knots after her other daily chores were done.

NINETEENTH CENTURY

Ipswich in the Nineteenth Century

Growth and change continued in the nineteenth century. New modes of transportation came to Ipswich as did new industries and institutions. The Ipswich Female Seminary and the Ipswich Mills Company were noteworthy additions to the life of the town. Ships sailed the coast under the watchful eye of Ipswich's own lighthouse, but sometimes suffered in the stormy seas. By the close of the century, streetcars rattled through Market Square and a homegrown artist shared Ipswich landscapes with the world.

❖

CHINA TRADER AUGUSTINE HEARD

The Ipswich-born sea captain and merchant Augustine Heard pursued interests from his own backyard to exotic ports of call. His later life included philanthropy at home, such as donating an organ to First Church and establishing the town library. While these altruistic activities were no doubt satisfying, they were nowhere near as exciting as some of his adventures farther afield.

He was the fifth child of John Heard, a shipping merchant with his own wide interests; these included importing molasses from the West Indies for his Ipswich distillery and privateering during the American Revolution. Augustine went to sea at the age of twenty aboard a merchant vessel bound for Calcutta. As the ship's supercargo he was responsible for trading and selling the cargo when the ship reached port, a job for which he possessed a natural talent. Soon the young man made a reputation for himself and became a captain.

After more than twenty profitable years on trade routes to the East and West Indies and the Mediterranean, Heard chose to retire and return to Ipswich, where he wasted no time getting involved with business ventures. He invested in the short-lived lace factories in the 1820s, then underwrote the Ipswich Manufacturing Company, which made cotton cloth. Heard didn't linger in Ipswich to take a hand in these operations, because in 1830 he became a partner in a trading company and sailed for China.

By 1840 he had established his own trading firm, Augustine Heard and Company, with an office in the port city of Canton at the mouth of the Pearl River. The company engaged in the legitimate trade of Chinese tea and silk and New England cotton. It also traded in opium, transporting it from Turkey and India for illegal sale in China.

During the Opium War, Chinese and British forces did battle while companies from the United States (which remained neutral) tried to carry on business as usual, but the violence often engulfed them as well. Between 1840 and 1842 Heard's offices and warehouse were burned three times. In one attack Heard and his staff, including his nephew John, were besieged and found themselves running low on ammunition just as the mob was about to force its way into the building. They managed to slow their attackers, many of whom were barefoot, by breaking all the bottles they could find and covering the floor of a passageway with glass as they made their escape.

Several years later, Heard retired to Ipswich where he died in 1868. Artwork and other items that he brought home from China are in the museum collection at the Heard House. Built by Augustine's father, the house is now owned by the Ipswich Historical Society. It is open to the public.

❖

Open to interpretation

In January 1814, the death of a forty-nine-year-old Ipswich woman became a hot topic for temperance-minded gossips. Rumor had it that she perished due to spontaneous human combustion brought about by overindulgence in alcohol. A less spectacular explanation—and one far less graphically instructive to indulgers—was that she had burned to death when a candle tipped over and ignited her bedclothes.

Grave-robbing

Sally Andrews died of consumption on Christmas Day 1817 at the age of twenty-six. She was not married, and her parents, brothers, and sisters buried her and mourned their loss. As the winter passed they found little peace; after visiting her resting place in the wintry cemetery, they had the uneasy suspicion that something—something unspeakable—had occurred. They were afraid that she had been taken from her grave.

When spring finally came to Chebacco parish, Sally Andrews's family had their suspicions confirmed. Several other families who had lost relatives that winter also began to wonder, and it was discovered that eight bodies in all had been taken from their coffins in the graveyard. The victims who had been buried that winter were of all ages and descriptions: two ten-year-old boys; Andrews and a thirty-five-year-old woman; and three men aged twenty-four, sixty-five, and seventy-eight. The eighth victim was an elderly man who had died several years earlier.

The horrific news spread like wildfire; handbills expressed the village's outrage. One leaflet described the horror poetically in "Lines on a Recent Inhuman, Barbarous and Atrocious Affair Perpetrated in Chebacco" and described the "wretched monster" who had robbed the graves "for the sake of gain and filthy lucre."

Several months later the eight empty caskets were re-interred in a common grave following a service at the Chebacco church, offered by the Reverend Robert Crowell. He condemned the grave-robbers as well as the individual who had put them up to it. By this time, the identity of that individual was coming into focus, and Crowell was pretty direct in pointing a finger when he declared in the memorial sermon, "If a single soul is hardened in sin by the practice of stealing dead bodies, the evil thus occasioned must infinitely outweigh all the good which the science of anatomy ever did or ever will do to the bodies of men."

The perpetrator was Thomas Sewell, the local doctor, who had used the bodies for anatomical research. He was charged with the crime, fined heavily, and asked to leave the area. In 1819, Sewell, with his wife and young son, moved to Washington, D.C., where he had a distinguished career as a physician and professor at a medical college. Sewell's wife left behind family in Essex, including her sister, Mrs. Robert Crowell, the minister's wife.

The Reverend Mr. Crowell went on to write a book on the early history of the town of Essex, but in it Sewell's crime is nowhere mentioned.

Smuggling and stocking machines

In the late eighteenth century, Britain had a monopoly on the manufacture of hosiery. To discourage the development of the industry in other countries, the British government imposed a prohibitive duty on the export of textile machinery, which had been developed in England. In 1818, violators faced a stiff fine of five hundred pounds for exporting a machine to make stockings.

Benjamin Fewkes and George Warner were stocking makers from Nottingham who wanted to emigrate to the United States, but in order to ply their trade in a new land with any success, they needed one of these highly prized stocking frames. They purchased a used machine without difficulty and took it to a framesmith, asking him to put it in good working order. Getting it to America was another matter. Smuggling it out of England was their only option, so they took the machine apart and carefully packed the pieces into two boxes, which were hidden in the loose salt cargo of a brig bound for America. The hidden crates went undetected by British customs officers as the ship left port. Off the coast of Massachusetts, a schooner met the brig as planned, and the two boxes were removed from their hiding place, transferred to the schooner, and delivered to Boston on September 4, 1818.

Fewkes and Warner took the crates to Watertown and began reassembling the stocking frame only to discover that one piece, the sinker bar, was missing. They wondered if the framesmith in England had purposely sabotaged their scheme, but they had little time to stew about it. Warner set his mind to contriving something to replace the lost part and soon had a workable substitute.

In 1822, Fewkes purchased a house in Ipswich and the two installed their machine in his kitchen, where they began turning out machine-knit stockings. Other weavers, displaced from the Nottingham factories, soon joined them with more smuggled equipment. The machines could be used not only for knitting stockings but also for producing lace, a discovery that transformed the tradition of Ipswich lace making.

The Boston and Ipswich Lace Company was started with investments from Joseph Farley, Augustine and George Heard, and William Sumner. Dr. Thomas Manning, John Clark, Ammi Smith, and several others followed suit with the New England Lace Company. During the 1820s, many of the same women who had hand-worked lace with pins and pillows now plied their skills in these small factories, embroidering, mending, and washing machine-made lace. Boys wound the miles of thread. Men were the lace weavers. But the promise of a strong local industry was thwarted by international economics: Just as the British had imposed sanctions on exports of their machinery, they also imposed high duties on the export of the fine linen thread that was vital to the lace industry.

The manufacture of lace was abandoned, and the stocking frames and their operators returned to the making of hosiery. Until mid-century this industry existed on a small scale with "stockingers" plying their trades in their houses or small shops. In 1832, machinists James and Joseph Peatfield constructed two stocking frames—probably the first ones manufactured in this country—for the small factory Fewkes had established near his home (after the business outgrew the kitchen, no doubt).

The hosiery produced by machines was knit more coarsely than hand-knit stockings and therefore was looked down upon by some consumers. Many women refused to wear machine-made hosiery. But with the outbreak of the Civil War, there was a sudden demand for hosiery for the troops, and large-scale production at Ipswich's hosiery mills began.

Loads of timber that came down the Merrimack River bound for the shipyards of Essex floated down Plum Island Sound to the Ipswich River and through the canal.

THE SHORT-LIVED CANAL

Transportation moved on Ipswich waterways—ocean, rivers, and creeks—from earliest days. Moving materials, especially large heavy loads, by water was less cumbersome than overland transport. Practical minds quickly recognized the potential benefits of a canal across the marshes that would connect the Ipswich and Chebacco Rivers, and in 1652 the town voted to pay ten pounds to Thomas Clark and Reginal Foster to excavate a ten-foot-wide passage. Apparently, the town didn't get its money's worth because the canal wasn't completed. Another request for someone to attempt the job was made in 1682, still another in 1694, but there were no takers for the project.

Finally, in 1820 the Essex Canal Company was incorporated and a canal was cut from the Fox Creek branch of the Ipswich River to the Chebacco. The half-mile waterway across the marsh cost just under $1,100 to complete. Twenty-seven shares were sold for forty dollars each to cover the costs (shareholders received dividends of between 5 percent and 6 percent for the next thirteen years).

The canal was a success. Loads of timber that came down from the Merrimack River bound for the shipyards of Essex floated down Plum Island Sound to the Ipswich River and through the canal. Tolls were based on the type of cargo: oak timber rated at seventeen cents per ton, pine timber three cents less. Staves and hoops for barrels and hogsheads all had their own rates, as did shingles and clapboards.

Unfortunately, the successful enterprise was short-lived. The coming of the railroad, the decline of the wharves, and the shift in local industries all played a part in eroding the importance of the canal. Nearly two hundred years in the planning, it fell into disuse before the nineteenth century closed. Marsh grasses and shifting sand shrank the manmade waterway that had accommodated vessels loaded with lumber, and the canal now provides passage only for recreational travelers in kayaks, canoes, and powerboats.

RESTRICTIONS ON PEWS

As abolitionism became a hot political and social topic in the 1830s, the people of Ipswich found themselves divided on the question, despite the fact that slavery had been outlawed in Massachusetts for nearly half a century. One of Ipswich's ardent abolitionists was the Reverend David Tenney Kimball, minister of First Church from 1806 to 1857 and an outspoken advocate of immediate emancipation.

Supporting the abolition of slavery didn't necessarily mean supporting equal rights for blacks. When slavery was legal in Massachusetts, Ipswich slaveholders had encouraged their slaves to attend church, but they were relegated to the gallery and not allowed to sit in pews. This restriction continued even when the abolition-minded pastor Kimball was in the pulpit, and with the installation of pews in the galleries there may not have been any permissible place left for black churchgoers.

One bill for the sale of a new pew in the gallery, dated 1825, reads: "It is agreed between the said Parish and the said Michael Farley his heirs and assigns, that if he or they, or either of them shall ever hereafter sell or let said Pew to any Negro or colored person or persons, the same shall revert back to said Parish and successors and the title thereof become void according to the Conditions of the sale thereof."

❖

Educational pioneer Zilpah Grant

Influence depends more on character than on office.
Correction administered in anger has no effect either to
humble the scholar or to increase the influence of the teacher.
Make no contemptuous remarks concerning any of your pupils.

Zilpah Grant followed her own advice as a teacher and principal of the Ipswich Female Seminary. As both a product and a pilot of the movement for improved education of women which started in the 1820s, Grant and her compatriot, Mary Lyon, changed the face of women's education both in Ipswich and in the wider world.

Grant came to Ipswich from Adams Female Academy in Derry, New Hampshire. When she accepted the position, she wrote to her friend Mary Lyon, asking that she join her. Grant had high hopes but no illusions about her new employers: "The leading men in Ipswich wish to have a flourishing school there, partly because they wish that their building (which has cost four thousand dollars) may not be lost."

The large building, near the foot of Meetinghouse Hill, had been constructed two years earlier, but only an abortive attempt at running a school had been made. The energetic Miss Grant was exactly what the trustees were looking for in a principal for their new private seminary, and further testimony to her pedagogical abilities and inspiring personality was the group of forty students from Derry who followed her to Ipswich.

The first term opened in April 1828. The school grew steadily. For the first few years, an elementary level was offered, but it was soon phased out. The student body from then on ranged in age from fourteen to mid-twenties; many of the advanced students were young women who had already been working as teachers who wanted to learn the teaching methods practiced and preached by Grant and Lyon. Their belief was that all young women could benefit from the training, whether they put the training to use as teachers or governesses or mothers. As Grant summed up the purpose of her program of study: "The great object of the Seminary is not to finish but to commence education."

Young women interested in attending the Seminary had to complete an application that asked for "name, age, attainments, and moral character." Morality was a significant part of the program. The principal gave an address on "scripture truth" two or three mornings a week, church attendance was mandatory, and every carefully scheduled day included half an hour for silent reflection. Dancing was not included in the curriculum because it was deemed inappropriate for a practical education, but calisthenics were required to develop physical discipline. Early on, Grant led the calisthenics class herself, but she tore a tendon in her leg; the injury ultimately caused her retirement ten years later.

By 1839, more than fourteen hundred students had attended the Ipswich Female Seminary for at least one term. There were 488 teachers and 21 missionaries among them. Mary Lyon had left in 1834 to establish another school, Mount Holyoke Seminary, which would become Mount Holyoke College. Another teacher and graduate, Eunice Caldwell, departed Ipswich to become principal of Wheaton Seminary, later Wheaton College.

After Grant's health forced her to retire, the school closed for several years. It reopened under the guidance of John P. Cowles, a professor from Oberlin College, and his wife, one of those 488 teachers. Eunice Caldwell Cowles and her husband ran the school until its closing in 1876.

❖

WRECK OF THE *DEPOSIT*

December 14, 1839, continued the stretch of unseasonably mild weather that had marked the first half of the month. As keeper of the Ipswich Light, T. S. Greenwood manned his post at the edge of the sea as usual. In the early hours of Sunday, December 15, the mild conditions ended abruptly as winter blew in with a vengeance. All day Sunday and into Monday snow, rain, and wind pounded the coast with hurricane force.

Through the thick weather Greenwood did not see the schooner just off shore as it bucked wildly upon the waves and drew nearer and nearer to Ipswich beach around midnight. The *Deposit* was out of Belfast, Maine, captained by a man named Cotterell. This would be his last voyage.

The schooner ran aground on the shoals off the beach in the dark of the early morning. Solid land was tantalizingly close, but the churning surf barred the ship's crew, Captain Cotterell, and his wife from reaching safety. As the waves washed over the deck of the schooner everyone took to the rigging. Hours of exposure, the exertion of clinging to their precarious holds, and the emotional strain of the seemingly endless ordeal began to take their toll. Two of the crew, one of them just a boy, succumbed to the cold; their dead bodies lay unquietly on deck as the ship continued to rock with the storming sea.

At daybreak the survivors saw a man appear on the beach. They screamed for help with what strength they had left and must have been sorely disheartened when he ran away from the ship and up over the dunes. The man, whose name was Marshall, returned a short time later with Greenwood and a lifeboat.

The two men stood on the beach and stared at the breaking surf between them and the ruined vessel, realizing that their tiny lifeboat didn't stand a chance in such waters. But the desperate screaming of Mrs. Cotterell overrode any logical argument, and Greenwood knew he had to take action. He tied one end of a rope around his waist and, as Marshall held the other end, plunged into the frigid water. The wind and waves pushed him back toward shore as he struggled to make headway, but finally he reached the wreck and clambered aboard. After Greenwood secured his end of the rope, Marshall tied his end to the lifeboat, waited for a lull in the waves, then pushed it into the water and jumped in. Greenwood hauled Marshall and the dory alongside the *Deposit*.

Greenwood first lowered Captain Cotterell, completely exhausted and barely conscious, into the lifeboat. Just as Marshall got him settled, a great swell filled the tiny boat and tossed both men into the surf. Marshall resurfaced, but the weakened captain drowned. Greenwood threw Marshall a rope and pulled him on board. The lifeboat was lost.

The rescuers seemed as stranded as those they had hoped to aid. They waited several hours as the storm died down and the tide receded. Another young sailor, weakened by the ordeal, expired. Mrs. Cotterell was hysterical at having witnessed her husband's drowning, but she was carried to safety in the strong arms of Marshall and Greenwood; they held her tightly between them and rode the swells of the waves into the beach. In the end, only two of the crew survived and made it to shore by floating on a piece of what used to be their schooner. Greenwood and Marshall took the survivors—George Emery, Chandler Mahoney, and Mrs. Cotterell—to the nearby house of Humphrey Lakeman, an old sea captain, where they were tended to with food and warmth while they awaited the doctor.

When word of the wreck reached town, other folks made their way to the beach to help recover the four bodies, and two days later funeral services were held at South Church. Sixteen sea captains served as pallbearers.

❖

THE FATE OF THE *FALCONER*

Wind and snow and tragedy blew in with another fierce December storm in the year of 1847. A brig called *Falconer* was on her way from Cape Breton Island to Boston laden with 350 tons of coal, and a crew and passengers totaling fifty-three. Many of the passengers were emigrating from the island to the United States, hoping to improve their luck and their lives. Through the poor visibility of the stormy night, Capt. Joseph Rolerson spied the beam from Annisquam Light at Gloucester, but he mistakenly identified it as Cohasset Light. The captain adjusted his course, then realized his miscalculation when the lighthouses of Ipswich and Newburyport came into view. Now he knew he wasn't off Cohasset, but he wasn't sure where he was. He ordered some of his men to drop the anchors (the *Falconer* was about three miles off shore) to ride out the storm or until daylight might permit him to determine his location.

The storm continued to rage as the unseen sun rose and set and night fell again. When the next day dawned, the gale was unceasing in its assault of the ship. The force of the wind and sea uprooted the brig from her anchors and felled her masts like trees. The battered vessel, pushed before the might of the waves, struck a shoal and stuck fast about a quarter mile off the beach. The collision and the continued pounding by the waves weakened the damaged ship, and she began to take on water through numerous leaks.

The passengers evacuated the flooded cabin and joined the crew on deck, where everyone faced the threat of being washed overboard. Most lashed themselves to the rigging of the ruined brig, praying that if they managed to keep from being thrown into the sea, they would also survive the cold winds and icy spray. Seven men tried instead to brave the sea in the brig's lifeboat—the boat was swallowed by a monstrous wave before it reached the beach. Three of the men were drowned, but four struggled up from the surf to dry land.

Humphrey Lakeman, who had helped victims of shipwrecks before, saw the floundering brig from his house near the beach and sent word to town. Wagons full of people willing to help, bearing blankets and other aid, hurried through the snow to the shore. They gathered and looked in despair at the daunting surf between the beach and the wreck. They could barely make out the figures on deck through the falling snow.

William Chapman couldn't just stand there. Perhaps the young sailor was thinking that, with a different twist of fate, he could be one of those figures stranded on the sinking ship. Impetuously, he grabbed a small dory that had been deserted on the beach, slid it

William Chapman rowed fiercely, fighting to reach the brig even as his own little boat took on water.

into the sea, and jumped aboard. He rowed fiercely, fighting to reach the brig even as his own little boat took on water. He drew alongside the larger vessel and pulled himself up onto the deck as the dory disappeared out from under his feet and sank from view.

Despite—or maybe because of—the foolhardiness of his seemingly one-way trip, the survivors on the *Falconer* took encouragement from Chapman's feat. And some of the men on shore took inspiration from it: they ran to the lighthouse for more boats. The chore of hauling the boats across nearly two miles of soft sand from the lighthouse to the beach closest to the wreck was nothing compared to the effort of rowing the boats back and forth through the churning surf as the volunteers toiled to bring the survivors as well as the bodies of those who perished safely to shore.

Thirty-six survivors were embraced by the waiting townsfolk, who wrapped them in warm blankets or their own warm coats when supplies ran low and helped them to Captain Lakeman's house where they could recuperate out of the elements. Many were suffering the effects of their long exposure to the cold. Captain Rolerson was among the survivors, but he was very weak and lived less than an hour after the rescue; the bodies of his wife and son were among those recovered.

In all, seventeen people lost their lives in the wreck of the *Falconer*. Most of the bodies found were taken to Town Hall where a funeral was held. Captain Rolerson had been a member of the Odd Fellows, so the local lodge took responsibility for returning the bodies of the captain, his wife, and son to their relatives in Belfast, Maine. Twelve of the dead were buried in a common grave in the High Street burying ground, where a stone commemorates their passing and their names.

❖

READ ALL ABOUT IT

On Friday, October 12, 1866, readers picked up the first edition of the *Ipswich Bulletin*. Its publishers offered a subscription to the paper for one dollar per year and were confident that the new publication would "meet with a hearty welcome, and become a regular visitor to many firesides in town." The slogan beneath the front-page banner proclaimed "Devoted to Temperance and Literature." This motto may have proved too limiting—or perhaps too off-putting to readers and potential advertisers—because all subsequent issues featured the slogan, "Devoted to the best Interests of our People."

The inaugural issue included a front-page poem about a local landmark, "The Legend of Heart-break Hill" (the only local flavor on page one) as well as the tale of "A Woman's Heroism," chronicling the determined efforts of the invalid wife of a Union army general to go to the aid of her husband at Fort Sumter. A considerably shorter piece mentioned the exploration of Popocatépetl, a volcano in Mexico, with an eye toward extracting its large deposits of sulfur.

Inside news stories covered the fiftieth anniversary of Mr. and Mrs. Joseph Conant and the Republican caucuses in both Ipswich and Essex. A report from the Committee of Arrangements for the Fourth of July celebration disclosed its expenses for the festivities, which included $200 for fireworks, $13.75 for lumber to construct tables, and $176 to hire the band. Other items of local interest: an announcement that Capt. Augustine Heard had purchased land on which to build the town a public library; abundant crops of potatoes, corn, pears, and apples as well as high prices for salt hay; and the purchase at auction of the Farley estate by the Ipswich Hosiery Company, "who we understand contemplate making alterations in the building, converting it into a boarding house for their operatives." Improvements around town included enlargements of Mr. Robert Jordan's store on Market Street and the net factory owned by Mr. James S. Glover, who was also in the process of installing steam apparatus to power the looms. The paper also reported that, as of October 1, the Ipswich House of Correction, which had just been enlarged by twenty cells, had 87 inmates (62 males, 25 females) with 38 committed during the month of September and one transferred to the State Lunatic Hospital.

The *Bulletin* carried other news from beyond Ipswich. In a prominent position on page two, the text of a proclamation by President Andrew Johnson recommended that Thursday, November 29, be set aside as a day of thanksgiving and that "on the same solemn occasion we do humbly and devoutly implore Him to grant to our national councils and to our whole people that Divine wisdom which alone can lead any nation in the ways of all good." The Treasury Department had "completed the settlement of the prize money made at the capture of Mobile" with Admiral Farragut being rewarded a share of $19,000. A Virginia bricklayer escaped injury after a three-story fall when a fellow worker looked up and saw him falling, then caught him in his outstretched arms. A 78-year-old woman in Bath, Maine, had spun over one hundred pounds of yarn in the previous month.

The columns of advertisements touted a variety of cures, boots and shoes, wood and coal, and sewing and knitting machines. One sought "500 bushels of Bayberries for which cash will be paid." The coffin warehouse in Damon's Block advertised the availability of rosewood, walnut, and pine among its stock. And D. M. Tyler promoted "Watches, Jewelry & Silver Ware. Also a general assortment of 8 day and 30 hour clocks."

The four-page paper was printed every other week by the publishers of the *Gloucester Telegraph*, but its visits to the town's firesides lasted only a year. The final edition of the *Ipswich Bulletin* appeared on Friday, September 27, 1867.

ROYAL LINEAGE

Jacob Safford was working in Ipswich as a butcher and a farmer in the 1870s when he noticed a beautiful young woman named Emma Jane Mitchell. She had come to town with her mother selling baskets, but it wasn't the finely crafted weaving that got his attention. He introduced himself. They courted. They married on New Year's Day, 1873. Theirs was an interesting union of royal lineage.

Emma was a princess of the Wampanoag tribe, a direct descendant of Massasoit on her mother's side. Her father, Thomas, was a Cherokee who worked as a steward on a merchant ship out of Boston. Her mother, Zerviah, was left to raise eleven children when her husband died in the 1850s. (Later in her life, Zerviah Mitchell co-wrote a book to help preserve her heritage; *Indian History, Biography and Genealogy* was published in 1878.)

Jacob's grandfather had come to Ipswich as a slave of the Safford family. Everyone called him Prince and believed from the stories he told that he really was of regal blood. The stories said his family ruled a tribe in Africa, where he was kidnapped by slave traders and thrown into a ship bound for America. Prince attained his freedom, and in 1780 he married a woman named Kate, who was then a slave of Joseph Cogswell. Prince retained the Safford name, and he and Kate remained in Ipswich and raised their family. Among their children was a son named James who married Peely Cheever; together they had two children, Jane and Jacob.

While most of the black families slowly disappeared from Ipswich as succeeding generations moved away, the Safford clan remained deeply rooted in the community. Jacob had lived in the same house his whole life, and it was there on Green Street that he and Emma raised their family. They had four children—Helen Gould, Alonzo Cheever, Emma Cheever, and Zervia Estelle. Alzono died as a young man, and none of the daughters married, so sadly, the royal lineage they carried from both sides of their family tree went no further.

Daughter Emma was the last surviving member of her family, and in 1948 she erected a stone in the cemetery on High Street as a memorial to her family. Her name was added to the monument when she died in 1958.

COASTING TOWARD THE WRONG SIDE OF THE LAW

In the editorial column of the *Ipswich Chronicle* on January 15, 1881, the editor cautioned readers of the dangers of sledding down Town Hill, especially during business hours. The boisterous young coasters on their double-runner sleds, building momentum on the slope of the hill as they whizzed toward Market Square, could do considerable damage to pedestrians or a horse and sleigh (not to mention themselves) in the likelihood of a collision.

The editorial was precipitated by a news item reported in the same edition: Seven young men had been arraigned in court for violating the town bylaw that prohibited sledding on Town Hill. The boys—among them George Schofield, who in ten years' time would be editor and publisher of the *Chronicle*—claimed they had permission from Mr. Sayward, the chairman of the board of selectmen. When the chairman appeared at the arraignment, he allowed that there may have been some miscommunication; he had told the boys that he personally didn't object to coasting, but that his personal opinion didn't alter the prohibition. In view of the possibility of a misunderstanding, the case against the seven was discharged on the promise that they stay out of further trouble.

That didn't mean that other youngsters and other sleds would not cause problems. Just a few days later William Rust was knocked off his feet by an out-of-control sledder on a downtown sidewalk. Rust hit his head in the fall, and the unidentified but certainly frightened boy ran away. Passersby discovered the unconscious man a short time later and took him home. Except for a bloodied head and no recollection of the accident, Rust was fine. The hit-and-run sledder was not apprehended.

❖

STEAMSHIP WRECK

Emerson's Rocks near the southern end of Plum Island have proved hazardous to many a ship navigating this stretch of the New England coast. One such unfortunate craft was the steamship *City Point* which ended her career in the early hours of May 21, 1883. The sidewheel steamer, owned by the Hathaway Steamship Company of Boston, was making a regular run from Annapolis, Nova Scotia, to Boston carrying thirty-one passengers and a cargo of potatoes, halibut, and eggs.

The *City Point*, with a crew of twenty-four under the command of Capt. O. Ludlow, had left Annapolis Saturday evening five hours behind the scheduled departure time and in heavy fog. The thick weather persisted as the steamer made her way down the coast. Ludlow's course setting should have put the ship several miles outside Thachers Island, but his compass may have been wrong or the prevailing current into Ipswich Bay may have been running stronger than usual. The close veil of fog cut visibility to a few hundred feet, and neither captain nor crewmen saw the silhouette of Plum Island looming to starboard nor the rocks just ahead. The pilot was listening for the Thachers Island foghorn but what he suddenly heard instead was the sound of breaking waves.

Steamships like the *City Point* were not best suited for ocean running. The vessels, high and imposing with their broad paddlewheels and tall smokestacks, were constantly buffeted by winds, and components of the paddlewheels could be damaged in rough waters. Slowed by these inherent handicaps, steamships often had to run in adverse weather to compete with faster sailing vessels.

At 3:30 A.M., near low tide, the 204-foot *City Point* ran aground on Emerson's Rocks. Full reverse on the engines arrested the steamer's momentum, but only enough to ease the collision, and they couldn't pull her loose once she had run aground. Crew and passengers stayed on board until daybreak, when all of the passengers and some of their luggage were successfully evacuated to the beach (except for a slight dousing in some cases). As the tide rose the waves pounded the steamship's damaged hull, cracking her open like one of the eggs she was transporting. Much of her cargo floated off on the waves and was scattered along the beach for a mile.

Word of the wreck reached Ipswich around 9 A.M., and the *Carlotta* made her way to the site of the disaster. The *Carlotta* may have appeared to be an unlikely heroine. She was a much smaller steamer that plied the waters of Plum Island Sound twice a day, usually carrying passengers bound for seaside outings to points from the Parker River to Little Neck to Grape Island. But the perky little excursion boat was up to the task; she occasionally took on extra duty as a tow boat.

Capt. Nat Burnham piloted the *Carlotta* alongside the ruined bulk of the *City Point* to find that all of the passengers and crew were safe—one young woman was busily spreading the wet contents of her clothes trunk on the beach to dry—and needed only to be conveyed to the mainland.

Though the *City Point* was destroyed, the wreck occurred with no injury or loss of life. Recovered cargo and the remains of the vessel, including the steam machinery, were sold at auction. Passengers and crew continued their journey to Boston, taking the train from Ipswich.

❖

THE ARTIST AMONG US

As an artist and teacher, Arthur Wesley Dow put Ipswich on the cultural map. The Ipswich Summer School of Art, which he founded, flourished around the turn of the twentieth century. The irresistible local landscapes that Dow captured on canvas also drew other painters to the area. But in his early days as an artist, Dow

Arthur Wesley Dow and his French connections caused a stir in Ipswich.

was looked on by some of his fellow townsfolk as an oddity rather than an icon.

His young life had been steeped in the good old New England ways. Born in 1857, he first attended school in Ipswich then went on to the Putnam Free School in Newburyport where he was valedictorian of the class of 1875. His father's tight financial straits precluded college, but bright, young Arthur taught elementary school in Linebrook parish and continued his own studies under the tutelage of the Reverend John P. Cowles, the retired schoolmaster of the Ipswich Female Seminary. He also began to sketch many of the old houses around town and to illustrate a serial dedicated to local history called the *Antiquarian Papers.*

At the age of twenty-six, Dow took the opportunity to study art in France. He returned to Ipswich five years later a changed man. He had embraced French ways—the art, the fashion, the language—and appeared out of place in his hometown. He continued to wear his beard closely trimmed, which gave him a European air, and rarely appeared without his beret. He rented a downtown storefront to use as a studio and outfitted it in the style of his artistic workspaces in France. No doubt, Ipswich pedestrians often walked by and peeked in the windows at the foreign-looking artist in his Continental surroundings who, strange as it must have seemed, was a native son.

Dow and his French connections caused a stir in Ipswich once again in the year 2000—seventy-eight years after the artist's death—when the school committee considered selling two Dow landscapes to help defray the costs of a new performing arts center. The two oils on canvas had been painted by the artist in France for exhibition at the Paris Salon of 1889; they were given by his widow to the Ipswich School Committee to be displayed in the schools. Both had hung in a variety of school locations for years before the committee proposed selling them. After much negative response, the committee abandoned the idea, and in April 2001, the two paintings, on loan from the school committee, were hung in the public library.

FIRE!

In the earliest hours of January 15, 1894, a night worker at the Boston & Maine Railroad depot noticed a bright light toward Central Street. Moments later he sent out the alarm for fire. The three-story Jewett's block, where the fire broke out, was already blazing, and soon the fire spread to all the buildings along the side of Central Street from Hammatt to Market Street. The bitter wind fanned the conflagration, and the single-digit temperatures made difficult work for the firefighters. Doused by the splashing of the hoses, their clothes froze upon them as they worked. Townsfolk turned out with hot drinks to fortify the hosemen and other fire-fighters—and to watch in horror as a large part of the downtown area was consumed by flames.

Ipswich firefighters battled the spreading blaze as their hoses froze and reservoirs of water, first near the library then near the town pump, played out. Finally, Ipswich Mills provided a power-ful source of water, pumping from the mill's fire hydrant, which allowed the firemen to get the fire under control. Crews from Salem arrived after daybreak and drew their water directly from the river, and the collective effort succeeded in dousing the flames by midafternoon.

Even before the smoke had cleared, the issue of a town water supply (which had been a point of contention for some time) re-emerged as a hot topic of conversation. The following issue of the *Ipswich Chronicle*, which ran an extensive front-page account of the blaze complete with woodcut illustrations, included an edito-rial by publisher George Schofield urging creation of a town water system, so that the hosiery mill wouldn't be the only site of a hydrant.

The *Chronicle's* competitor, the *Ipswich Independent*, had no detailed coverage of the tragedy; the *Independent's* office was located on Central Street and had been destroyed in the fire, along with all of the company's records and files. The most recent issue of the paper had been sent to the post office but not mailed, and the postmaster allowed the *Independent* staff to retrieve the copies in order to rebuild the subscription list. George Schofield also offered the use of his printing equipment until the *Independent* could establish new offices, so that the paper wouldn't have to suspend publication.

In the aftermath of the devastation a special town meeting was called to vote on the water question. On February 19, the town voted 472–78 for the installation of a municipal water system.

The work did not come soon enough. On April 20, just three months after the Central Street blaze, another downtown fire near Depot Square completely destroyed Damon's block and badly damaged businesses in Lord's block as well. The fire spread from a back room of the Provision Market and quickly engulfed the neighboring furniture store, hairdresser's, clothing store, variety store, and the Salvation Army. Once again firefighters ran hoses from the Ipswich Mills to extinguish the blaze.

Another town meeting was held three days later. Although voters had endorsed the idea of a municipal water system, they still had to approve the means to pay for it. In the weeks after the first vote there had been speculation that the appropriation of funds would not get the two-thirds of the vote necessary to pass. The Damon's block fire underscored the dire threat faced by the town, and the hard lesson would not need to be repeated a third time. The measure passed with a vote of 306–110. Construction proceeded swiftly, and the town showed off the new hydrant system with a demonstration on Thanksgiving Day, just seven months later.

❖

STREETCARS

The opening of the Gloucester, Essex & Beverly Street Railroad line from Essex Junction to Market Square in the summer of 1896 offered new mobility to residents and visitors alike—to the south at least. Then in 1900, the Georgetown, Rowley & Ipswich Street

Railway Company laid its tracks from the north to Ipswich, completing what should have been an unbroken route for electric streetcar travel from Haverhill and Newburyport to Cape Ann, Beverly, and beyond. Yes, it should have been.

The glitch in the system was right in the heart of Ipswich. The line from Rowley ended on High Street on the north side of the Boston & Maine Railroad tracks. The Essex line extended its tracks from Market Square out to High Street, and it was hoped that the Boston & Maine would allow the street railways to build a crossing over their tracks. The railroad resisted a crossing, and the bridge over the tracks wasn't constructed until 1907. Until then, passengers on the electric streetcars rode to the High Street terminus of either line, then exited the car, walked across the railroad tracks, and boarded a waiting car on the other side.

This minor physical inconvenience was nothing compared to the financial quagmire in the early days of operation. Controversy raged in 1900 because the two streetcar companies were not issuing transfers from one line to the other for patrons whose trips continued within Ipswich as they had agreed to do; travelers were often charged twice. The two companies could not agree on what percentage each should get of the five-cent fare, and they reached an accord only after Ipswich selectmen threatened to report the trouble to the state railroad commissioners. Trouble erupted again over transfers for school children who only paid half-fare, but in order to avoid further difficulty, the president of the Georgetown, Rowley & Ipswich streetcar company decided to let school-bound children ride his line for free and then issue transfers to the Gloucester, Essex & Beverly cars at his own expense.

TWENTIETH CENTURY

IPSWICH IN THE TWENTIETH CENTURY

In Ipswich's fourth century many aspects of the town's life seemed to echo issues of the past. European immigrants struggled to carve out a new life in a new home, and people fought for the right to worship in the church of their choice. Both institutions and architecture set in place by the town's founders survived into twentieth-century life. Echoes of an even more distant past sounded with the discovery of archeological evidence of the area's earliest inhabitants.

❖

THE LIGHTS COME ON

After the town water system proved a success, a plan for an electric power plant gained popularity. In April 1903, Ipswich appropriated $25,000 for the project, a price tag that bought: the plant constructed next to the water pumping station; the dynamo, engine, and related materials at the plant; transformers; 891 poles; 635 streetlights; and 20 miles of wire. On the evening of Wednesday, November 18, with everything in place, the dynamo was started for the first time. Suddenly, the incandescent lamps glowed brightly and pushed back the dusk from streets all over town to the surprise and delight of everyone who witnessed the sight. The new lighting system passed its first test brilliantly.

❖

THE HOUSES THAT CRANE BUILT

When Richard T. Crane Jr. purchased property at Castle Hill in 1910, he built a lavish summer home, an Italian Renaissance–style villa, with lawns, terraces, a sunken garden, and a variety of lesser buildings that complemented the mansion in style and created an elegant enclave. Sweeping views of the marshes with the ocean beyond completed his real-life canvas.

Crane was a plumbing magnate whose father had made the family fortune by manufacturing pipe fittings for industrial use. The younger Crane expanded the family business, moving into the manufacture of plumbing fixtures. His business objective? "To make America want a better bathroom." Crane, as one of the wealthy of America's Gilded Age, wanted a palatial summer mansion so that he could display his wealth and relax with his family. He spent the summers in Ipswich with his wife Florence and their two children, Cornelius and Florence.

Mrs. Crane never did warm to the Italianate house. Despite the sixty-five rooms, she found it lacking. Her indulgent husband asked her to give it a chance for several years, and if she still didn't like it, he promised to build her a new one. Apparently, her feelings didn't change, because in 1925 Crane razed the mansion.

The Cranes' second Ipswich home, an English manor completed in 1927, didn't match the property's other buildings, but it suited Florence better. The rotunda of the Great House even featured a homey touch: the ceiling mural included likenesses of Richard, Florence, and the children, as well as two maids and a favorite pet cat. The new home had fifty-nine rooms, among them, of course, plenty of bathrooms with Crane fixtures.

By happy coincidence, at about the same time the first house was demolished, the Methodist Episcopal Church was in need of a new heating system. With a charitable view on Crane's part and a waste-not, want-not attitude on the part of the church, the slightly used boilers were salvaged from a dump on the Crane property and installed in the church basement.

The house itself became a charitable donation when Florence Crane bequeathed it to The Trustees of Reservations upon her death in 1949 (Richard had died just three years after the second mansion was completed). Cornelius and his wife Mine later donated the rest of the Crane acreage to The Trustees. More than 2,100 acres, all open to the public, include Castle Hill, Crane Beach, and the Crane Wildlife Refuge. The Great House was designated a National Historic Landmark in 1998.

❖

CABLE MEMORIAL HOSPITAL

Richard Crane chatted away with his friend Benjamin Cable as they rolled along Linebrook Road enjoying the crisp air of late September. The roar of Crane's car made the cows in the fields raise their heads. People in 1915 were getting accustomed to the sight of automobiles on the roads, but the cows still didn't know what to make of the odd, oversized creatures.

Crane steered around several curves and across the intersection of Linebrook with the Newburyport Turnpike. The sound of another automobile registered in his consciousness just before the collision.

At that startling moment of impact, Dr. David Edsall watched the front end of his touring car smack Crane's broadside, sending it rolling. Edsall's wife in the seat beside him pitched forward toward the windshield as the car came to an abrupt halt. Crane's automobile made nearly two complete rolls before it came to rest.

Other motorists stopped to help the accident victims. Dr. Edsall seemed fine, although his wife was complaining of pains in her leg. Crane had been held in the driver's seat by the steering wheel and the high seat back; he emerged from the wreck badly shaken with an injured shoulder. Rescuers discovered Cable pinned beneath the car, unconscious. Benjamin Stickney Cable, who had served the nation as assistant secretary of commerce and labor in the administration of William Howard Taft, was rushed from the scene to the downtown office of an Ipswich doctor, where he was pronounced dead.

Crane mourned the loss of his friend with an important act of philanthropy, the funding of Cable Memorial Hospital. Fund-raising for a hospital had actually been started several years earlier by a small group of teenagers known as the Hospital Girls. These members of the Manning High School class of 1912 decided in their freshman year to raise money to build a town hospital. In their four years of high school, the girls sold flowers and postcards, staged plays, and organized food fairs to support their plan. By graduation, they had raised one thousand dollars. More importantly, they had inspired adults of the town, who formed the Ipswich Hospital Corporation in 1910.

The hospital was still in its planning and development phase (although the town had purchased an ambulance to transport patients to Beverly and Salem) when Benjamin Cable died in 1915. With Crane's backing, the hospital moved swiftly from idea to reality. The building's cornerstone was laid in June 1916, and in August 1917 the new hospital opened with twenty-four beds, operating room, pathology lab, x-ray machine, and "etherizing" room. A bronze tablet memorializing Benjamin Stickney Cable was unveiled in the lobby.

Several additions to the building were made over the years, but in 1979 the hospital was unable to continue functioning as an independent facility and it was sold to Beverly Hospital. Doctors' offices, Cable Emergency Center, and the Cable Gardens apartment complex currently share the site.

❖

IPSWICH CLAMS

In early years, Ipswich landowners, known as commoners, had rights to common lands in proportion to their property holdings. Although the town's clam flats were originally designated as common lands, Ipswich commoners voted to give them to all inhabitants, so that every resident, landowner or not, could reap the benefits of clamming. For nearly 250 years the people of Ipswich harvested the shellfish primarily for bait; only the poorest residents resorted to eating them. But sometime after the Civil War people discovered what they were missing, and clams became popular fare. The 1912 Schofield Clam Law, named for Ipswich's newspaper editor and tenacious state representative, required the state, which had assumed control of Massachusetts clam flats, to lease that control to the town. The combination of the early commoners' foresight and the 1912 law put the flats in the hands of the town.

In order to act responsibly and thoughtfully in overseeing the flats, the selectmen appointed a committee to study the situation and make helpful recommendations, which they offered in 1916. The committee proposed a clamming commission to oversee the protection and cultivation of the flats; they also recommended a tax per barrel of clams to pay for that cultivation. There were seven recommendations altogether, but the gravest was the proposal to crack down on other places that claimed to have "Ipswich clams" by reporting them to the proper authorities.

Some listening to the report would have argued that it wasn't a clam's origin that made it an Ipswich clam but rather how it was fried. True Ipswich clams were fried just the way Honey Russell did it at Russell's Lunch. The Depot Square restaurant was renowned for its clams, and people often came to town on the train or the trolley with Russell's as their sole destination. Russell was particular about his clams and their preparation. He used only small, tender clams dredged in corn flour—not corn meal—and fried them at just the right temperature in lard. If they're done any other way, call the proper authorities.

STRIKE!

The 1913 strike at Ipswich Mills was not the first protest laborers here had staged, but it was the biggest, most contentious, and bloodiest. The clash was multidimensional—between workers and employers, between police and protesters, between natives and immigrants. The verbal volleys were as destructive as any bricks and stones.

The strike, over wages and working conditions, started in April (although the notion of a strike had wafted through town for at least a month before). The mill closed at noon on April 23. During the early weeks, the strikers were described by the local paper as orderly, and a speedy resolution to the stoppage seemed likely.

The mill reopened on May 21 with some of its regular work-force and some temporary workers. At opening time there were also a hundred police officers in the streets outside the mill—Ipswich officers as well as police from Beverly, Gloucester, Lynn, Marblehead, and Salem and state police in plain clothes. In addition, more than sixty of the mill's overseers were sworn in as spe-

When the mill reopened, there were a hundred police officers in the streets outside—Ipswich officers as well as police from Beverly, Gloucester, Lynn, Marblehead, and Salem and state police in plain clothes.

cial police. Strikers were banned from the streets closest to the mill, and two were arrested for disturbing the peace. Emotions ran high on both sides. It was reported that women strikers bit and scratched the police, while one special policeman struck and injured a man who had nothing to do with the strike—he was waiting for the trolley car to Rowley.

Tensions escalated over the following weeks as uncertainty mounted. At one point the strike seemed to be fizzling out as a growing number of workers returned to the mill. Then it was reinvigorated by rallies and rousing speeches by union organizers from the International Workers of the World (IWW).

Finally, on Tuesday, June 13, tension reached the breaking point. Picketers had gathered along Saltonstall Street to meet the exiting laborers at the close of the work day. Supporters lined the sides of the street watching the marchers. Policemen at the mill gates also watched. The confrontation was touched off as soon as the gates opened for the departing workers. Afterwards there was some dispute over just what and who had started the riot. One woman who was pushed from the crowd of onlookers into the street near the police was apprehended by the officers and arrested. Some said that did it. Others said an onlooker threw a rock at the guards.

No matter what started the altercation, the violence escalated quickly. In the confusion of people running into or away from the fray, fists flew, clubs swung, rocks and bottles hurtled through the air, and shots were fired. Twenty minutes later the melee was over. Six gunshot victims were rushed to Salem Hospital; scores of others received wounds from clubs and projectiles. Twenty-four-year-old Nicoletta Pandelopolou had been shot in the head and died two hours after the riot. Flora Cornelius, Panagiola Paganis, Staffis Jorokopolus, George Kalivas, and Arthas Paraskavas all recovered from their wounds. More than a dozen strikers were arrested at the scene, and three IWW representatives—Nathan Hermann, Carroll L. Pingree, and his wife Emma May Pingree—were arrested later and charged with inciting the riot, despite the fact that they hadn't been at the confrontation.

The next morning the out-of-town police were back in full force. Not a single picketer appeared at the mill gates. The atmosphere in town was both stunned and tense. Thomas Halliday, National Secretary of the IWW, arrived on a morning train and was arrested within moments for obstructing a sidewalk.

Strikers and organizers were arraigned at Ipswich District Court and the trials began immediately. Police testified that they had acted defensively; strikers vowed that police had fired the first shots and the fatal one. Prosecutors characterized IWW representatives as "craven-hearted individuals, strangers to honest labor" and charged them with the murder of Nicoletta Pandelopolou. As the likelihood grew that she had been killed by a policeman's bullet the murder charges were dropped.

The strike continued in an increasingly hostile atmosphere. The mill ordered the eviction of families living in eighteen company-owned houses. Strike meetings continued on the grounds of the Greek church, and several speakers were arrested a few days after the June 22 meeting for making comments "of such a nature as to warrant them being placed under arrest," as the *Ipswich Chronicle* put it. The selectmen voted to ban fireworks from the upcoming Fourth of July celebrations and also proposed to hold a public meeting to plan an especially patriotic Independence Day observance—as a lesson in Americanism for the strikers. In his weekly editorial column George Schofield warned Polish and Greek strikers against the dangers of communism. After the Fourth of July planning meeting, rumors flew that the meeting was actually to organize vigilantes to drive the IWW representatives out of town.

The Fourth of July came and went. The intended patriotic instruction was useless since strikers boycotted the ceremonies. The strike dragged on for several more weeks while court cases were concluded. Ipswich strikers broke with the IWW, and the representatives packed their bags and left town. Strikers finally returned to work in late July without their pay raise. But the shots fired and hateful words spoken could not be taken back. There was little satisfaction on any side.

THE FLU EPIDEMIC OF 1918

In early September 1918, newspapers in Ipswich reported developments in the Great War in Europe, Liberty Loan drives, and the collection of magazines, peach stones (used to make charcoal for gas masks), and other materials to support the war effort. It's possible nobody noticed at first when obituaries began announcing the deaths of young, previously healthy people after illnesses of only a few days.

The outbreak of Spanish Influenza, as it was mistakenly dubbed, came to Massachusetts early in what would become a worldwide pandemic when sailors aboard ship at Commonwealth Pier in Boston began exhibiting symptoms of the grippe in August. By the end of the month there were more than five dozen men sick, and just a few short weeks later that many men were dying each day of flu at the army hospital at Camp Devins. The symptoms were extreme for an ordinary strain of flu as victims turned blue and their lungs filled with fluid. The most common targets were young, stronger individuals rather than the old and infirm. Officials contacted the media in early September to warn people of a possible epidemic.

By late September the flu was making news in Ipswich. On September 20, Cable Memorial Hospital announced that visitors would be prohibited in an attempt to stop the spread of the flu. On September 24 it was reported that 150 mill employees were out sick (this number would climb to 470 in just two weeks). Each new edition of the newspaper contained several flu-related obituaries and reports of new cases of influenza. A house-to-house canvass on September 28 ascertained that there were 1,017 Ipswich residents down with the flu.

Public gatherings, such as the Liberty Bond drives, as well as heavily attended funerals contributed to the spread of the epidemic. Schools and theaters were closed indefinitely as of September 25. Other town organizations continued to post notices of activities in the newspapers until October 11, when a proclamation from the Board of Health in the *Ipswich Chronicle* declared a suspension of "all meetings of lodges, clubs and other organizations, and the closing of all bowling alleys, billiard and pool rooms, coffee rooms and soda fountains. Ice cream can be sold in cones and to be taken out but not to be eaten on the premises. All funerals must be private, only relatives being allowed to be present."

Although the newspaper optimistically reported that the worst of the epidemic seemed to be over, it included a page-one plea against circulating harmful rumors about the flu and its possible victims.

The hospital gave itself over fully to combating the epidemic. The board of trustees requested that a tent hospital be erected on the grounds to create more bed space for flu sufferers. On October 6, Company N, Fifteenth Infantry, of the State Guard erected fifty tents. The guardsmen set up two facing rows of two-person tents with board walkways and floors, trenches for water pipes, and wiring for electricity to service the tent hospital, which was named Camp Mason, after hospital president Herbert Mason. Flu and pneumonia cases were transferred from the hospital building to the tent facilities, and pneumonia patients from Rowley were also moved to Camp Mason. A large, temporary wooden building, erected by federal officials as a hospital for servicemen, also appeared on the Cable Memorial grounds.

Further spread of the epidemic produced some unusual pronouncements of vigilance. One newspaper piece reminded readers of the contagious nature of the flu strain with the catchy slogan, "Coughs and sneezes spread diseases" and proclaimed that those sneezes and coughs could be "as dangerous as Poison Gas Shells." Notices posted around town warned that anyone caught spitting in public would be fined.

As the epidemic wound down, life in Ipswich began to return to normal. The men of Company N started breaking down Camp Mason's tents a brief two weeks after they went up; remaining patients were treated in the temporary federal building. Churches and movie theaters reopened the third week of October, and schools were back in session a week later. By October 25, the *Ipswich Chronicle* was reporting happier statistics—the Liberty Loan subscriptions, even in the midst of the epidemic, totaled $432,400, well exceeding the quota of $344,000—and the Local News column contained announcements of a variety of organizations' upcoming activities, including a public dance at the Knights of Columbus Hall.

❖

DEMON RUM

In Prohibition-era Ipswich, the rural landscape provided plenty of places to conceal a still, and the maze-like marshes were perfect for rum-running boats. That there was a certain amount of illicit trade going on residents didn't deny (after Prohibition was repealed, of course), and every once in a while even the officials knew about it.

Prohibition agents converged on Bull Brook Farm on Linebrook Road one Monday night in September 1927 and seized a 150-gallon still, 50 gallons of distilled liquor, and 1,700 gallons of mash to make plenty more. The agents, along with several state police officers, apprehended the owner of the farm, Kate Kocincki, and her son. Another man, Anthony Robbins, was caught operating the still. A fourth man, the aptly named Sam Stillman, drove up to the house with a supply of sugar and yeast and several empty containers in his car only to find himself in the middle of a raid. All four were arrested and charged with unlawfully engaging in the distilling of spirits.

Not all of the liquor that made its way to Ipswich in the 1920s and early 1930s was the homemade variety. Shortly after midnight on June 25, 1930, firemen investigated what seemed to be a small blaze in the marshes not far from Little Neck, where someone had used the new firebox to sound the alarm. What they found at the scene was a well-equipped rum-running boat in flames. They

In the morning, house and moving crew faced the challenge of crossing the Choate Bridge.

summoned the police, who confiscated 87 cases of Scotch and 290 bottles of champagne. Although it seemed a significant amount, it certainly hadn't filled the high-speed craft to capacity. Authorities theorized that the rum runners disabled the vessel by accidentally ramming a sandbar off Treadwell's Island and managed to unload a portion of the cargo before setting the boat afire and making their escape. Further contraband was probably spirited away by local residents who spied the abandoned rum runner before the police and firemen arrived.

❖

FIRST PERIOD MOBILE HOME

On a Thursday in December 1927, Market Street offered a most unusual sight: The Whipple House moved slowly along the pavement as though some giant turtle had decided to carry a house upon its back. The historic home, built in stages by three generations of John Whipples starting in the mid-1650s, was departing its original location near the corner of Topsfield Road and Saltonstall Street just outside Depot Square for a placid spot overlooking the south village green.

The move sparked controversy. Some questioned the reasoning behind the Historical Society's decision to relocate the building from its original lot. Yes, over the centuries the mills had sprung up like weeds just a stone's throw away and the old house now stood amidst tenement housing for the workers rather than beside more spacious lots owned by men with names like Appleton and Denison, as it had in earlier times. But even if the surroundings had changed, there was much to be said for the integrity of the original setting. The house itself was rare even among First Period houses because, although it was built in stages by succeeding owners, all of the construction was completed in the First Period (1630–1700) without later structural additions.

Many in the Historical Society argued that the building, which had been purchased by the organization in 1898 for restoration and use as a museum and meeting place, attracted little notice in its urban setting, while lack of parking discouraged visitors. And, they said, the village green at the bend of South Main Street was pleasant looking and within sight of tourists traveling on Route 1A who could easily park and engage themselves in this wonderful piece of history.

The argument raged on. William Sumner Appleton, a member of the Historical Society and corresponding secretary for the Society for the Preservation of New England Antiquities, spoke out against the move. He was one of a list of illustrious and knowledgeable signers of an article outlining opposition to the plan. William's cousin, Col. Francis Randall Appleton Jr., was also a member of the Historical Society; he favored the relocation, and the two hotly debated the issue at Society meetings. After a published letter of protest, the dispute continued in the newspaper with an editorial in the *Ipswich Chronicle* accusing the signers of the letter (the ones with "the alphabetical display after their names") of never even having been to Ipswich to find out the reality of the situation. Before the Society purchased it, the editorial explained, the house was "utterly neglected" and a "disreputable tenement."

Despite the protests, the Society went ahead with the relocation. On December 15 the building movers of the B. F. Goodwin Company raised the house from its original foundation. The ancient chimney stack and a lean-to at the rear had to be dismantled for the move (just as the protesters had feared). Still, while the action appalled some observers, from an engineering standpoint it was amazing. The house rested on enormous timbers with rollers underneath. A large truck towed it ever so slowly. Telephone and electric crews took down low-hanging wires in the house's path. By evening, the Whipple House reached Market Square, where it settled down to spend the night. In the morning, house and moving crew faced the challenge of crossing the Choate Bridge, where Goodwin ordered his men to jack up the building high enough to clear the stone sides of the bridge. The old house rolled across the river to a new neighborhood.

The Whipple House, a National Historic Landmark on South Village Green, is still owned and maintained by the Ipswich Historical Society. One of the oldest museum houses in the country, it is open to the public three seasons of the year.

❖

Disappearing lighthouse

The shifting sands of time played a major part in the life of Ipswich Light. The first light, constructed in 1838, was a range light (a pair of beaacons on square towers positioned so that when ships' pilots lined up the two lights, they knew they were sailing in midchannel). Blowing sand eroded the mortar in the two brick towers, and in 1873 a forty-five-foot cast-iron tower replaced the main light. A new bug light (the smaller of the two beacons) was also installed. The guidance was helpful to navigators, but the ever-shifting channel required repositioning the lights seven times before the end of the century.

The migrating sand dunes didn't erode the iron tower, they engulfed it. Finally, the lighthouse keeper could no longer enter the tower through the door, which had disappeared, and gained access only through a second-story window. A revolving light was installed in the main tower in 1903 and the position of the bug light adjusted two more times before it was dismantled in 1932. At this time the main light, which had been electrified, went unmanned, and a long tradition of lighthouse keepers in Ipswich ended.

In 1938 the Coast Guard announced that it would move the sand-besieged cast-iron tower to Edgartown Harbor on Martha's Vineyard. Despite protest by Ipswich residents, the move went ahead. In early 1939 the Ipswich lighthouse departed on a truck bound for Chelsea; there it was loaded onto a barge and transported to its new assignment on Martha's Vineyard, where it remains on duty in 2001.

❖

Top secret

Few people knew the identity of the component that was being manufactured at the Sylvania plant in Ipswich starting in 1942. Observers could see that the windows of the factory were barred and painted black and that the buildings were watched by armed guards. Employees knew that they had to pass a background check, take an oath of secrecy, and not venture out of their own departments (colored badges identified where each employee was allowed to go). Rumors abounded, but everyone was confident that the work that had transformed a mild-mannered lighting company into a production plant for a top-secret gizmo was contributing to the war effort.

The object of all this secrecy was the proximity fuse, a device originally developed for use in anti-aircraft shells. The fuse, placed in the nose of a missile, sensed when the shell was close enough to its target to detonate. The proximity fuse made direct hits unnecessary and would become a vital piece of the Allies' defense against Japanese aircraft in the Pacific as well as the defense of London against German buzz bombs.

All of this was unknown to the hundreds of women and girls who worked six days a week at the plant during the war years. At the peak of production Sylvania employed twelve hundred people manufacturing twenty-five thousand fuses per day.

Digging into the past

Just as Ipswich is enriched by the legacy of its early English settlers, it also abounds with evidence of much earlier habitation. A site near Bull Brook, discovered in 1950 by several amateur archaeologists, contained a treasure trove of artifacts left behind by Paleo-Indians about ten thousand years ago.

Joe and Nick Vaccaro of Beverly and their friend Bill Eldridge from Lynn, all members of the Massachusetts Archaeological Society, were on a typical weekend outing when they eyed the recently bulldozed section of a gravel pit off Paradise Road. It looked like a promising spot to poke around, and once they had asked permission from the owner, the trio split up and began their individual operations. When they regrouped for lunch, Joe shared a treasure he had found. The large projectile point was an interesting specimen, although Joe was disappointed that one of the barbs had been broken. It reminded Bill of a picture he had seen in a book.

The friends showed their find to a professional archaeologist who confirmed that it was, just as Eldridge suspected, a Clovis point—a spearhead used by the inhabitants of this region between ten and twelve thousand years ago. Beyond providing confirmation, the professionals of the field didn't pay much more attention to the point or its amateur discoverers. They didn't believe there was anything else at Bull Brook to uncover.

Eldridge and the Vaccaros disagreed, and they—along with two more Vaccaro brothers and friend Antonio Orsini—continued to explore the gravel pit. The friends kept digging, devoting more time and effort to the project than any professionals could afford, eventually working the site for more than twenty years.

As it became obvious that the initial discovery was just the tip of the iceberg, the professional community acknowledged the importance of their find. Over the years, the Bull Brook dig produced over ten thousand stone tools. The amateur archaeologists recovered projectile points for arrows and spears, scrapers for cleaning hides, gravers for poking holes and scoring surfaces, hammerstones for fashioning other tools, and even stone drills shaped quite similarly to modern drill bits. The tools were clustered in forty spots—forty dwelling sites of Ipswich's earliest residents—some still showing evidence of fire pits and remnants of meals of beaver and caribou.

After testing some of the artifacts, archaeologists determined that Bull Brook was the oldest known site of habitation on the

New England coast. Its wealth of tools is one of the largest collections of Paleo-Indian artifacts in North America. In order to share them with the public, the group of friends donated their stone treasures to the Peabody Essex Museum in Salem.

❖

FIRE ON THE HILL

In the midst of a thunderstorm on June 13, 1965, lightning struck the roof of the Congregational church. The first alarm sounded at 4:30 P.M., followed by a second alarm ten minutes later as fire and smoke began to engulf the Gothic outlines of the stately church on Meetinghouse Hill. Firefighters from Ipswich and ten surrounding towns answered the call to battle the stubborn blaze that left the historic building a gutted shell.

The fifth church building to stand on the site, it had been constructed in 1847 but included relics of its predecessors. Some—like the rooster weathervane perched atop the steeple and like the tower clock, the oldest still in use in the country—survived the fire. Concerned and curious townspeople gathered at the scene, and many participated in a hasty effort to recover some of the items from the church before they were destroyed by fire, smoke, and water. The organ, a gift from Augustine Heard, and the desk used by the Reverend David Tenney Kimball from 1806 to 1857 were among the pieces rescued. An eighteenth-century pulpit and sounding board which had stood in the previous building (and had been stored away in the belfry when the Gothic church was built) were brought out later, having suffered minimal damage.

The wooden Gothic church, which had been even more distinctive for several decades in the early 1900s when it was painted red, soon disappeared from its familiar place in the Ipswich landscape when its remains were taken down. Construction of a new church took place in 1970, and the sixth meetinghouse of the First Church of Ipswich rose in the traditional spot atop Meetinghouse Hill, overlooking the devil's footprint and the rest of the town.

❖

THE LIGHTS STAY ON

The evening of November 9, 1965, was pretty typical in Ipswich. Everyday family activity unfolded as darkness fell: the streetlights came on to guide husbands on their way home from work, wives prepared supper on their electric ranges, youngsters listened to their record players or watched television. By the time everyone sat down to the dinner table they were well aware that this wasn't a typical evening in most places around New England.

Shortly after 5 P.M., the power grid serving the northeastern United States and much of eastern Canada collapsed. The cause was difficult to pin down, but the effect was obvious: as the relays that controlled various parts of the system got the message that there was no outside supply of electricity available, they shut down their own system generators rather than burn them out under too much demand. One by one, just as though some giant hand had flipped a series of light switches, cities of the Northeast went dark. Toronto at 5:15. Rochester at 5:18. Boston at 5:21. New York City at 5:28. More than thirty million people in New England, New York, and eastern Canada were left in the dark.

Back to the typical night in Ipswich: it was business as usual on the streets, in the homes, and at the Ipswich electric department. Ipswich and Rowley were two of the bright spots in Massachusetts because the electric plant serving the two towns had been set up to operate independently. In some instances Ipswich families set an extra place or two for supper or put on another pot of coffee as friends and relatives from nearby towns affected by the blackout dropped in for a hot meal and a well-lighted visit.

❖

PURITANS AND GOLF CARTS

A visitor to Hog Island in the late summer and early fall of 1995 may well have wondered what era it was—the First Period buildings, the ox carts, the wool-clad Puritans all seemed to suggest that it was 1692. Accusatory pointing fingers, a group of hysterical girls, and more than one uneasy individual taken into custody further attested that there might be witches about.

The seventeenth-century village, the outfits, and the hysteria were all courtesy of Hollywood—a 20th Century–Fox production of Arthur Miller's *The Crucible*. Many of the villagers were regular, non-Hollywood folk from in and around Ipswich, filling in as extras.

The island, once home to generations of the Choate family and now owned by The Trustees of Reservations, normally saw infrequent visitors, but that summer the scenic spot tucked into the river between Ipswich and Essex was abuzz with activity. By the time shooting began in early September a seventeenth-century village had appeared by (movie) magic. Stone walls meandered through the fields as though they had been there for years, rail fences zigzagged up the hills. A somber-looking meetinghouse stood amidst a small enclave of Puritan homes; the construction materials included decidedly non-Puritan fiberglass, and most of the buildings were mere shells, but the appearance was bewitchingly real. Fields of corn and stacks of hay, ox carts, sheep, goats, cows, and chickens gave the village more pseudorealism. At the bottom of the hill, with the marshes spreading in the background, stood the gallows, a focal point of the tale.

In powerful contrast to the pastoral set and period props was the equipment of moviemaking that constituted a second village on the island. Trailers filled with lighting apparatus, cameras, and costumes; portable dressing rooms (for the stars), portable toilets, and a giant commissary tent; tractors, trucks, buses, and golf carts—every single piece of it had been transported to the island by boat.

The images of behind-the-scenes action were worthy of their own movie: Puritan women in wool skirts and cotton bonnets perched upon a golf cart; young extras (some skipping school) rolling down the grassy hill during breaks; rows of men sitting under the careful hands of hairdressers, who placed their wigs just so; crowds of extras baring their teeth to the makeup staff, who painted many an incisor yellow for the sake of dental authenticity.

By November all the hysteria had been captured on film, from the exterior scenes on Hog Island to the jail scenes in a crude, cramped prison constructed near Castle Hill to the trials in the meetinghouse. (Through the creative geography of movies, the interior of the meetinghouse was actually a set built inside the old United Shoe factory in Beverly.) Then the film's cast and crew packed up their lights and cameras and took the action elsewhere. The local extras brushed their teeth and returned to their twentieth-century lives.

❖

KEEPING THE FAITH

The influx of immigrant workers to the Ipswich mills in the late nineteenth and early twentieth centuries had brought new cultures and languages to town. There were large numbers of French-Canadian and Polish workers, most of them Catholic, who wanted the stability and security of religion in their new homes. They found a Catholic church already established in town, St. Joseph's, which had been built by the mainly Irish-Catholic community in 1873. The challenge of learning a new language and the desire of both immigrant groups to preserve cultural aspects of their religious life prompted each to apply for recognition of a separate parish. In 1908, the Polish community constructed the Church of the Sacred Heart. The French-Canadian Catholics celebrated mass in the Damon Building until their church, St.

Stanislaus, was completed in 1911. And so the single parish that started the twentieth century quickly became three.

Fast-forward to 1996: the Catholic archdiocese of Boston announced that Ipswich's three parishes, totaling forty-five hundred people, would be merged into one congregation in June 1997. The archdiocese cited declining church attendance and a shortage of priests, especially those who could serve ethnic parishes.

Fiercely loyal Sacred Heart parishioners balked at the plan and launched a campaign to preserve their church. A dedicated group took out newspaper ads and spearheaded a crusade of letter-writing to the archdiocese. Signs pleading "Save Our Church" sprouted on lawns all over town. Masses and prayer vigils added to the efforts, but despite the Polish community's persistence, the merger went ahead as scheduled and services at the new parish began. Unwilling to give up as long as any avenue remained untried, Polish parishioners continued their crusade: They met with Bernard Cardinal Law to ask him to reconsider, appealed to their state legislators, and sought advice from a lawyer in Rome specializing in canon law. After Cardinal Law refused them, they petitioned the Vatican, and after their first petition was denied, they made a final appeal to the Vatican's highest court, the Supremo Tribunale della Segnatura Apostolica. The efforts, which stretched into 1999, were gallant but futile.

The new parish, Our Lady of Hope, began holding services at what had been St. Joseph's on Linebrook Road in July 1997. The three parishes of Ipswich, which had existed side by side for more than eighty years, became one.

❖

WHAT'S A FEOFFEE?

"Feoffee" is not a word in everyday use in the vast majority of cities and towns in the United States, but it endures in Ipswich. The fifteenth-century term has to do with property and money—

in the case of Ipswich, money for the town's schools. In 1650 the town's leaders, committed to the value of education, set aside an expanse of land to be leased out in perpetuity, the income to be used to support the Ipswich Grammar School, which prepared young men with all the Greek and Latin and other disciplines needed to enter the colony's new college called Harvard.

This 350-year-old pronouncement brought into existence what is now the oldest land trust in the country, overseen by the feoffees, or the trustees of the land grant. Since that time the land has been leased, and the money has gone to the support of Ipswich's schools. The schools have expanded—from a one-room affair to the whole of Ipswich's public school system—while the land has shrunk. The original grant described all "that Neck beyond Chebacco River and the rest of the ground up to the Gloucester line" which included Castle Neck and much of the land that became the town of Essex. The portion that remains under the guidance of the feoffees of the twenty-first century is the property on Little Neck. The use of the leased lands has evolved from farming and grazing to summer vacationing and year-round living, but the responsibility of the feoffees has remained the same.

Tradition dictates that there be four feoffees. When there is a vacancy on the board, due to death or departure from town, the new feoffee is chosen by the other three. Tradition also dictates that the three "elder" selectmen serve as voting feoffees at the annual meeting. Modern-day feoffees, unclear whether that meant the three oldest selectmen or the three selectmen with the most seniority, solved the problem by giving each of the five selectmen three-fifths of one vote.

Finally, pronunciation is vital; it's no fun using unusual words when you're uncertain how to say them. The word is "feff´-ee." It doesn't rhyme with "coffee."

❖

SOURCES

Beattie, Donald W., ed. *Hamilton, Massachusetts: Chronicle of a Country Town.* Hamilton: American Revolution Bicentennial Commission, 1976.

Belknap, Henry Wyckoff. "Ipswich Indians Protected by a New England Good Samaritan." *Essex Institute Historical Collections,* Vol. LXVIII, No. 4. Salem: The Essex Institute, 1932.

Black, Robert C., III. *The Younger John Winthrop.* New York: Columbia University Press, 1966.

Bowen, Harold. *Tales of Olde Ipswich,* vols. I, II & III. Reprinted by PDA Publications, Ipswich.

Caldwell, Lydia A. "Our Honored Seminary." 1903.

"Catalogue of the Officers and Members of the Ipswich Female Seminary." Ipswich Female Seminary, 1834, 1836, 1839.

"Choate Bridge." Ipswich, Mass., 1901 (Reprinted from the *Boston Evening Transcript,* August 7, 1888.)

Clancy, Jane. "Castle on the Hill," *Colonial Homes,* August 1993.

Cook, George Allan. *John Wise: Early American Democrat.* Columbia University, New York: King's Crown Press, 1952.

Cotterell, Marta M. "The Laces of Ipswich, Massachusetts: An American Industry, 1750-1840." *Textiles in Early New England: Design, Production, and Consumption.* Boston: Boston University Press, 1999.

Crowell, Robert. *History of the Town of Essex from 1634 to 1868.* Published by the Town of Essex, 1868.

"Cultivation and Protection of Clams." Report of Committee. Ipswich: G. A. Schofield & Son, 1916.

Cummings, O. Richard and Gerald F. Cunningham. "The Haverhill, Georgetown & Danvers Street Railway– Georgetown, Rowley & Ipswich Street Railway System, 1900-1906." *Transportation Bulletin,* No. 67. August 1962-February 1963.

Cutler, William Parker. *Life, Journals and Correspondence of Rev. Manasseh Cutler, LLD.* Cincinnati: Robert Clarke & Company, 1888.

"Dark Days." *The Essex Antiquarian,* Vol. III, No. 4. Salem, Mass.: The Essex Antiquarian, 1899.

Davenport, Hazel Streeter. "The Devil In New England." *Yankee.* May 1958.

Davidson, Donald W. *Lighthouses of New England.* Secaucus, NJ: Wellfleet Press, 1990.

"Earthquakes in Essex County." *The Essex Antiquarian,* Vol. VI, No. 4. Salem, Mass.: The Essex Antiquarian, 1902.

Emerson, Everett, ed. *Letters from New England: The Massachusetts Bay Colony, 1629-1638.* Amherst: University of Massachusetts Press, 1976.

Felt, Joseph B. *History of Ipswich, Essex, and Hamilton.* Ipswich: The Clamshell Press, 1966.

Franklin, Benjamin. *The Autobiography and Other Writings.* New York: New American Library, 1961.

Goodell, A. C. "A Biographical Notice of the Officers of Probate for Essex County from the Commencement of the Colony to the Present Time." *Essex Institute Historical Collections,* Vol. III, No. 1. Salem: The Essex Institute, 1861.

Hart, Albert Bushnell, ed. *Commonwealth History of Massachusetts,* vol. I. New York: The States History Company, 1927.

Hartley, E. N. *Ironworks on the Saugus.* Norman: University of Oklahoma Press, 1957.

Hill, Sarah J. and Harry B. Hill, Jr. *Yankee City . . . Faces From Our Past,* vol. 1. Newburyport Five Cent Savings Bank, 1982.

"The Hosiery Industry of Ipswich, 1822-1922." Ipswich: Ipswich Mills, 1922.

Hurd, D. Hamilton, ed. *History of Essex County, Massachusetts,* vols. I and II. Philadelphia: J. W. Lewis & Co., 1888.

"Ipswich: Proud Settlement in the Province of the Massachusetts Bay." Charles E. Goodhue, Jr. New York: The Newcomen Society in North America, 1953.

Jameson, E. O. *The Choates in America, 1643-1896.* Boston: Alfred Mudge & Son, 1896.

Jedrey, Christopher M. *The World of John Cleaveland.* New York: W.W. Norton & Company, 1979.

Johnson, Arthur Warren. "Arthur Wesley Dow: Historian, Artist, Teacher." Ipswich Historical Society, 1934.

Keenan, Alice. *Ipswich Yesterday,* vol. II. Ipswich: Shanachie Publishing, 1984.

Lawson, Kenneth E. *George Whitefield's Ministry in Northern New England.* Dracut, Mass.: Northeastern Bible Institute, 1997.

Layton, Thomas N. *The Voyage of the "Frolic": New England Merchants and the Opium Trade.* Stanford, Cal.: Stanford University Press, 1997.

"Lombardy Poplars." *The Essex Antiquarian,* Vol. II, No. 4. Salem, MA: The Essex Antiquarian, 1895.

Martin, Wendy. *An American Triptych: Anne Bradstreet, Emily Dickinson, Adrienne Rich.* Chapel Hill: The University of North Carolina Press, 1984.

Mears, Sherman R. *The Essex Electrics: Streetcars in Essex, Massachusetts, 1895–1920.* Essex: Essex Historical Society, 1980.

Moffett, Frederick C. *Arthur Wesley Dow (1857–1922).* Washington, DC: The Smithsonian Institution Press, 1977.

Perley, Sidney. *Historic Storms of New England.* Salem: The Salem Press, 1891.

Pulsifer, Janice Goldsmith "The Cutlers of Hamilton." *Essex Institute Historical Collections,* Vol. CVII, No. 4. Salem: The Essex Instutute, 1971.

Richards, Allen Grant. "Rum Running on the Ipswich and Merrimack Rivers." *North Shore Life.* February/March 1990.

Robinson, Enders A. *The Devil Discovered: Salem Witchcraft 1692.* New York: Hippocrene Books, 1991.

Records and Files of the Quarterly Courts of Essex County Massachusetts, vols. 1-9. Salem: Essex Institute.

Snow, Edward Rowe. *The Lighthouses of New England.* New York: Dodd, Mead & Company, 1973.

———— *Storms and Shipwrecks of New England.* Boston: Yankee Publishing Company, 1943.

———— *True Tales of Terrible Shipwrecks.* New York: Dodd, Mead & Company, 1963.

"The Spirit of Ipswich." A Publication of the Bicentennial Committee of Ipswich, Massachusetts, 1976.

Story, Dana A. *The Shipbuilders of Essex: A Chronicle of Yankee Endeavor.* Gloucester, Mass.: Ten Pound Island Book Company, 1995.

"Three Hundred & Fifty Years of Ipswich History." Compiled by Elizabeth H. Newton, Alice Keenan, Mary P. Conley. Three Hundred and Fiftieth Anniversary Committee of the Town of Ipswich, 1984.

Van Dorp, Will and Linda Lee. *Incomplete Journeys.* Rowley: Rowley Press, 1989.

Vital Records of Ipswich, Massachusetts, Vols. I & II. Salem: The Essex Institute, 1910.

Waters, Thomas Franklin. *Ipswich in Massachusetts Bay Colony, 1633–1700.* Ipswich Historical Society, 1905.

———— *Ipswich in Massachusetts Bay Colony, 1700–1917.* Ipswich Historical Society, 1917.

———— A Sketch of the Life of John Winthrop the Younger. Ipswich Historical Society, 1900.

———— *Thomas Dudley and Simon and Ann Bradstreet, A study of house-lots to determine the location of their homes.* Ipswich Historical Society, 1903.

Weare, Nancy V. *Anne Bradstreet, America's First Poet: Selections From Her Works.* Newburyport: Newburyport Press, Inc., 1998.

Wells, Gwenn, "Essex County B.C." *Essex Life.* Summer 1983.

White, Theodore H., "What Went Wrong? Something Called 345 KV," *Life,* vol. 59, no. 2, November, 19, 1965.

"Zilpah Grant and the Art of Teaching." Recorded by Eliza Paul Capen. New England Quarterly, Vol. XX, 1947.

Peabody Essex Museum collections. Bull Brook exhibit at the Salem Visitor Center.

Frequently consulted: Ipswich Bulletin, Ipswich Chronicle, Ipswich Independent, Ipswich Observer, Ipswich Today, Newburyport Daily News, Newburyport Herald, Beverly Times, Boston Globe, Boston Herald, and the reference folders of the Ipswich Library

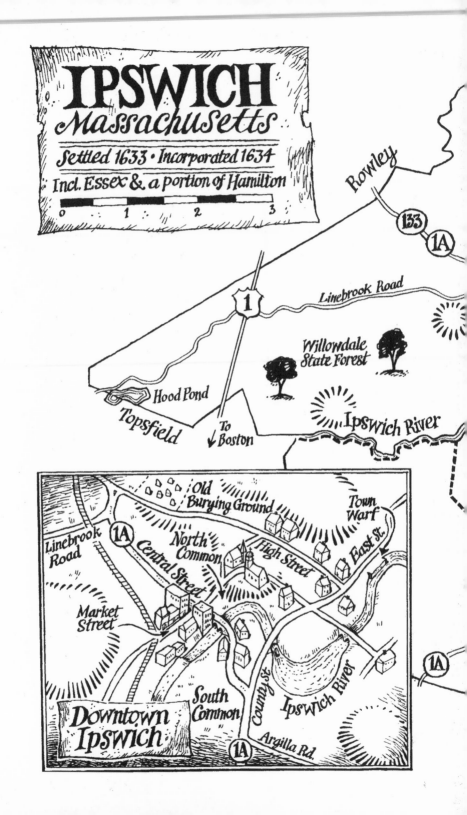

A Note to Parents and Caregivers:

Read-it! Readers are for children who are just starting on the amazing road to reading. These beautiful books support both the acquisition of reading skills and the love of books.

 The PURPLE LEVEL presents basic topics and objects using high frequency words and simple language patterns.

 The RED LEVEL presents familiar topics using common words and repeating sentence patterns.

 The BLUE LEVEL presents new ideas using a larger vocabulary and varied sentence structure.

 The YELLOW LEVEL presents more challenging ideas, a broad vocabulary, and wide variety in sentence structure.

 The GREEN LEVEL presents more complex ideas, an extended vocabulary range, and expanded language structures.

 The ORANGE LEVEL presents a wide range of ideas and concepts using challenging vocabulary and complex language structures.

When sharing a book with your child, read in short stretches, pausing often to talk about the pictures. Have your child turn the pages and point to the pictures and familiar words. And be sure to reread favorite stories or parts of stories.

There is no right or wrong way to share books with children. Find time to read with your child, and pass on the legacy of literacy.

Adria F. Klein, Ph.D.
Professor Emeritus
California State University
San Bernardino, California

Editor: Christianne Jones
Page Production: Melissa Kes, Joe Anderson
Art Director: Keith Griffin
Managing Editor: Catherine Neitge
Editorial Consultant: Mary Lindeen
The illustrations in this book were done in watercolor.

Picture Window Books
5115 Excelsior Boulevard
Suite 232
Minneapolis, MN 55416
877-845-8392
www.picturewindowbooks.com

Printed in the United States of America.

Library of Congress Cataloging-in-Publication Data
Williams, Jacklyn.
Happy Easter, Gus! / by Jacklyn Williams ; illustrated by Doug Cushman.
p. cm. — (Read-it! readers. Gus the hedgehog)
Summary: Gus and friends "eggscitedly" prepare for the Easter egg hunt at the park with
the giant chocolate rabbit for first prize.
ISBN 1-4048-0959-7 (hardcover)
[1. Easter egg hunts—Fiction. 2. Schools—Fiction. 3. Hedgehogs—Fiction.]
I. Cushman, Doug, ill. II. Title. III. Series.

PZ7.W6656Hae 2004
[E]—dc22
                                                              2004023313

Happy Easter, Gus!

By Jacklyn Williams
Illustrated by Doug Cushman

Special thanks to our advisers for their expertise:

Adria F. Klein, Ph.D.
Professor Emeritus, California State University
San Bernardino, California

Susan Kesselring, M.A.
Literacy Educator
Rosemount-Apple Valley-Eagan (Minnesota) School District

PICTURE WINDOW BOOKS
Minneapolis, Minnesota

Gus and Bean raced through the park on their bikes. The town was having its annual Easter egg hunt. They did not want to be late.

This year, the prize for finding the most eggs
was a gigantic chocolate rabbit! Gus was
sure he was going to win. He had practiced
hiding eggs and finding them all year long.

"Knock, knock," said Bean.

"Who's there?" asked Gus.

"Lettuce," answered Bean.

"Lettuce who?" asked Gus.

"Lettuce hurry or we'll miss the fun," said Bean.

"Good one," laughed Gus.

Mr. Chase, the school principal, had been busy hiding eggs in the park all morning. At noon, a crowd of happy, noisy children gathered around him. Billy was there, impatiently waiting for things to get started.

"Knock, knock," said Bean.

"Who's there?" asked Gus.

"Harry," answered Bean.

"Harry who?" asked Gus.

"I hope we Harry up and start hunting for eggs," said Bean.

Before Gus could laugh, Mr. Chase made an announcement.

"First, we're going to play a game. Then, we're going to look for eggs," he said.

"Everyone choose a partner and line up for the
egg toss," shouted Mr. Chase.

Bean walked over and stood next to Gus.
Mr. Chase gave each pair of children an egg.

"Knock, knock," said Bean.

"Who's there?" asked Gus.

"Stan," answered Bean.

"Stan who?" asked Gus.

"Stan over there. I'll toss you the egg," said Bean.

Bean tossed Gus the egg. Gus caught it and tossed it back. "Knock, knock," said Bean.

"Who's there?" asked Gus.

"Quack," answered Bean.

"Quack who?" asked Gus.

"If we quack the egg, we'll lose," said Bean.

The children tossed their eggs back and forth. One by one, the teams dropped their eggs. Then, they dropped out of the game. Finally, there were only two teams left.

Bean tossed the egg to Gus.

"Hey, Gus," said Billy. "Don't forget to catch it."

Gus caught the egg and tossed it back to Bean.
"Very funny, Billy," said Gus. "So funny I
forgot to laugh."

"No fair, Billy," said Bean. "You're making us nervous." SPLAT! The egg slipped through Gus's fingers and landed on his shoe.

"You won't forget to laugh now," chuckled Billy. "Because it looks like the yolk's on you!"

"It looks like the winners of the egg toss are Billy and his partner," said Mr. Chase. "And now it's time for the EGGS-citing hunt! Before we begin, I want to EGGS-plain the rules. You have EGGS-actly fifteen minutes to collect eggs."

He held up a beautiful, blue basket. On a bed of bright green, plastic grass lay a gigantic chocolate rabbit wrapped in shiny gold paper.

"Whoever finds the most eggs, wins this EGGS-tremely wonderful prize. So, grab your baskets. Get ready! Get set! Go!" Mr. Chase shouted.

The children began to scatter. Billy shoved
Gus to one side. "Out of my way," he said.
"Winner coming through."

Gus spied an egg hiding in a big bush and
rushed toward it.

As Gus reached in the bush to grab the egg,
Billy jumped out from behind it.

"ROAR!" he yelled.

"Yikes!" shrieked Gus. He stumbled headfirst into the bush. Sharp, finger-like branches reached out and grabbed Gus and his basket. First, they poked Gus in the arm. Then, they poked a hole in the bottom of his basket.

Gus struggled free. Billy howled with laughter.
Gus made a face at Billy and headed off
and searched for more eggs. Billy followed
close behind.

First, Gus found a striped egg. He put it in his basket. It slipped out and rolled away. Billy grabbed it. Next, Gus found a spotted egg. He put it in his basket. It slid out. Billy snatched it up.

On and on went Gus, picking up eggs and putting them in his basket. On and on went the eggs, slipping and sliding back out. On and on went Billy, scooping them up and filling his own basket.

Gus got so excited looking for eggs, he did not notice he was losing them as fast as he was finding them.

"Five more minutes," announced Mr. Chase.

The children scampered around to be sure all the eggs had been found.

"Time's up!" Mr. Chase shouted.

The children headed back. On his way, Billy
spied one last egg. It was the biggest one yet!

"With this one, I'll win the prize for sure,"
he thought.

Billy tucked the egg under his arm and hurried on. Suddenly, he let out a loud holler.

"Eeeeeeeeeeeee-yikes!" he screamed.
"It's after me!"

Billy dropped his basket and ran. Hissing and honking, the mother goose ran after him.

"Everyone count their eggs," said Mr. Chase.
"Let's find out who the winner is."

Gus looked at his empty basket.

"What's going on here?" he grumbled. "It
looks as though my eggs are still hiding."

"Look what I just found," said Bean.

"My eggs!" shouted Gus. Bean handed Gus Billy's basket.

Gus counted his eggs. "I have ten," he said.

"Does anyone have more than ten eggs?"
asked Mr. Chase. No one did.

"Then the winner is Gus, with ten eggs!"
Mr. Chase said.

Everyone cheered. Mr. Chase handed Gus
the prize.

"Thank you," said Gus.

Just then, Billy ran past the crowd. The goose
followed close behind. Everyone laughed
and laughed.

"Knock, knock," said Bean.

"Who's there?" asked Gus.

"Orange," answered Bean.

"Orange who?" asked Gus.

"Orange you going to share your prize with your best friend?" said Bean.

More *Read-it!* Readers

Bright pictures and fun stories help you practice your reading skills. Look for more books at your level.

GUS THE HEDGEHOG

Happy Easter, Gus! by Jacklyn Williams

Happy Halloween, Gus! by Jacklyn Williams

Happy Valentine's Day, Gus! by Jacklyn Williams

Merry Christmas, Gus! by Jacklyn Williams

Looking for a specific title or level? A complete list of *Read-it!* Readers is available on our Web site: *www.picturewindowbooks.com*